DINÉTAH

DINÉTAH

an early history of the Navajo people

LAWRENCE D. SUNDBERG

with drawings by the author

SUNSTONE PRESS
SANTA FE
NEW MEXICO

ABOUT THE COVER:
The cover illustration portrays two major leaders of the Navajo people: Barboncito and Manuelito. It was drawn especially for the book by Alton Littleman. During my time in Kayenta, I knew Alton well, from the time he was a fourth grade student in my first class through early manhood, until his untimely death in 1988. Alton had much to live for. He was a gifted artist, an industrious student, an insightful individual, but most of all a good friend. I shall miss him always.

PHOTO CREDITS:
The photographs appearing in *Dinétah: An Early History of the Navajo People* are credited by title, date, photographer [if available], and contributing institution, adjacent to each reproduction throughout the text. I wish to express my appreciation for the contributions made by the agencies credited for the use of these historic images.

On Title Pages 3-4: "Navajo Shepherdess" Photograph by Pennington, Courtesy the Denver Public Library, Western History Department #08699

Book Design: Mina Yamashita

Printed in the United States of America

Library of Congress Cataloging in Publication Data

Sundberg, Lawrence D., 1952--
    Dinetah : an early history of the Navajo people / Lawrence D. Sundberg : with drawings by the author. -- 1st ed.
      p. cm.
    ISBN 0-86534-221-0 : $12.95
    1. Navajo Indians--History. 2. Navajo Indians--Social life and customs. I. Title.
E99.N3S94 1995
973' .04972--dc20   94-32959
                                     CIP

Published by Sunstone Press
      Post Office Box 2321
      Santa Fe, New Mexico 87504-2321 / USA
      (505) 988-4418 / FAX: (505) 988-1025
      orders only (800) 243-5644

TABLE OF CONTENTS

Foreword

Dinétah: An Early History of the Navajo People is the story of the Navajo people and their struggle for survival. It is also the story of how their culture changed from an early hunting and gathering band to a powerful pastoral nation and, through contacts with Pueblos, Hispanic settlers and the American military, how that culture shaped the history of the Southwestern United States.

I wrote Dinétah for my elementary Navajo students because I believed they should have a book that would let them study their own history in school, as well as the histories of Arizona and the United States. Although I was an outsider, I wanted the book to represent a Navajo point of view as much as the accepted historical point of view, so I used the Navajo people's own accounts whenever possible. It is, after all, their story. Occasionally my telling of events is different from those told by traditional Navajo people. I do not want my readers to think that I disagree with those accounts. I was simply not knowledgeable enough to write about them. I have great respect for traditional Navajo viewpoints and I express this respect by including some of them in the book. I also encourage my audience to read traditional Navajo tales of their history and culture. There are several appropriate books listed in the bibliography.

Dinétah: An Early History of the Navajo People is dedicated to the Navajo people and particularly to the Navajo school children I've worked with over the years. It is a small repayment for their kind help, understanding, and support.

Many institutions have made significant contributions to the text, and I would like to recognize and express my gratitude to them as well: The Arizona Historical Society Tucson, The Arizona State Museum, California State University Fullerton Oral History Program, The Colorado Historical Society, The Denver Public Library, The Heye Foundation Museum of the American Indian, Kayenta Public School District 27, The Museum of New Mexico Archival Library Santa Fe, The Museum of New Mexico Laboratory of Anthropology, The Museum of Northern Arizona, The National Archives, The Northern Arizona Pioneers Historical Society Flagstaff, Northern Arizona University Special Collections Library, Rock Point Community School, The Smithsonian Institution, The University of Arizona Special Collections Library, University of New Mexico Albuquerque Library Special Collections, University of Utah Libraries Special Collections, The Utah Historical Society, and The Wheelwright Museum.

L. D. Sundberg
Phoenix, Arizona
May 1, 1994

THE FIRST NAVAJOS

There are different stories about the first Navajo people. Traditional Navajo legends tell how First Man, First Woman, the Holy People, and all the animals of earth came up to this world from the different worlds below. Traditional Navajo history tells how the first Navajos were made, who made the first clans and the first hogan. They tell about how the Holy People fought against floods, monsters, and evil giants. These stories are exciting and important to the Navajo people. But scientists who study different cultures tell another story. They believe that one thousand years ago the first Navajos lived far to the north in western Canada. The first Navajo people belonged to an American Indian group called the Athapaskans, who lived in western Canada. They called themselves Dineh, or The People, and they probably spoke the same language as other Athapaskan groups.

The first Athapaskans lived in small hunting and gathering bands and spent most of their time searching for plants to eat, catching fish and hunting different animals. After many, many years, some Athapaskan bands began to migrate, or move away, from each other. Why did they migrate? Were there too many people and not enough land? Did they run out of food? Did they have to follow the herds of animals they hunted for meat? Scientists can only guess. No one really knows.

Many of the Athapaskans migrated southward and some settled along the Pacific Ocean. These bands still live there today and belong to the Northwest Coast Indian tribes.

Other Athapaskan bands, such as the first Navajos, migrated southwards across the plains and through the mountains. It was a long, slow trip, but the bands weren't in a hurry. When they found a good place to stay, they often lived there for many years. After they'd hunted and gathered all the food they could find, they packed their things and traveled on. For hundreds of years, the early Athapaskan bands followed the herds of wandering animals and searched for good gathering grounds.

Many scientists think that some Athapaskan bands first came into the American Southwest around the year 1300. Some settled

MAP 1: Athapaskan migration southward.

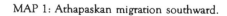

in southern Arizona and New Mexico and became the different Apache tribes. Apache languages sound very much like Navajo.

Like the Apaches, the Navajo Athapaskans found their own land and settled among the mesas, canyons and rivers of northern New Mexico. This first Navajo land was called Dinétah. Three rivers ran through Dinétah: the San Juan River, the Gobernador River, and the Largo River. Dinétah was just east of Farmington, New Mexico.

Life in Dinétah was full of work. Everything the people needed had to come from the land. The men hunted while the women and children spent most of their time gathering plants, seeds, and roots to eat. They also trapped small animals for food. Some scientists believe Navajos may have raised small amounts of corn as well. If a Navajo band was lucky, they might find enough food to last them several days. Then they could stop traveling and rest. But, before long, they would have to search for more. Sometimes good land was being used by another Navajo band and, since there wouldn't be enough food for two bands, one of them would have to move. The first Navajos probably did a lot of moving just to survive.

All food came from the land. At times, hunters would bring back a large animal they'd killed. Then the entire band would feast on roasted antelope or deer meat. More often, it was baked chipmunk, squirrel or prairie dog. Each day the people had to search for locusts, wild onions, wild potatoes, yucca and cactus fruits, different kinds of roots, and piñon nuts to eat. Sometimes they might not eat for several days!

Clothing came from the land as well. In the summer the first Navajos probably wore very little. Loincloths and skirts were made of buckskin, woven yucca, or juniper bark. They probably wore a pair of woven yucca sandals, too. For the winter there would be fringed buckskin shirts, buckskin leggings and a pair of tall, fur-

"Three children of Pesh-lakái-ilhiní," photograph by James Mooney (?), COURTESY OF THE SMITHSONIAN INSTITUTION NATIONAL ANTHROPOLOGICAL ARCHIVES, #2411

The first Navajo Athapaskan bands migrated southward from Canada for many years before arriving in Dinétah.

Winter wear of long ago.

lined moccasins. Mittens were made of wildcat fur and a soft rabbit skin blanket might cover the shoulders.

Tools such as axes, arrow heads, spear points, scrapers, choppers and knives were made from stone. Bowstrings, needles, and thread came from different parts of the deer or antelope. Clay was used to make brown cooking pots and yucca leaves to weave mats and baskets.

Navajo hogans, or dwellings, were much smaller in those days and easy to build. The first hogans were made of branches, bushes, a few mats, and earth. Besides these hogans, a band might have built a small shade for outdoor work and a sweathouse. They did not build large, earth-covered hogans because the first Navajos knew they'd have to move. People only took what they could put in their carrying bags. Everything else was left behind.

Early Navajo hogans might contain piñon pitch water baskets, a buckskin bag of bone and flint tools and a few pots filled with dried nuts and seeds. A quiver of arrows and a powerful sinew-backed hunter's bow might hang over the doorway. There'd be a yucca mat or an animal skin to sleep on and a small fire for cooking and warmth. In those days, Navajo bands moved so often they would own only as many things as they could carry.

An early Navajo family.

"Dinétah, New Mexico,"
photograph by the author

MAP 2: Dinétah and the
Four-Corners area.

THE PUEBLOS

Navajos living in Dinétah soon learned they were not alone. Imagine a cold winter day of long ago. A Navajo hunter is walking through the deep snow, following the tracks of a deer. After hiking up a steep canyon, he reaches a mesa top. The hunter follows the deer tracks until he comes to the mesa's edge. He stops to look down into a river valley far below. Suddenly the hunter spots something strange. Near the river he sees a village of square adobe houses that seem to be stacked on top of one another. The smoke of many cooking fires hangs over them. Through the smoke, the Navajo hunter can see people carrying bundles of firewood to their homes. The Navajo hunter has seen a village of Pueblo Indians.

In many ways, Pueblo village culture was different from Navajo band culture. Pueblo Indians belonged to many different tribes. They spoke different languages and they had been living in the Southwest United States for centuries. Most Pueblos lived in adobe villages scattered along the Rio Grande River in New Mexico. By the year 1400, there were over one hundred Pueblo villages in the Rio Grande River valley. Pueblo Indians were not hunting and gathering people. They lived in their villages year around and raised most of the food they needed. Pueblos planted large farms of corn, beans, squash and cotton along the banks of the Rio Grande River. They used the cotton they raised to weave colorful clothing.

After some time, many Navajo bands made friends with Pueblo villages and they began trading with each other. The Navajos traded animal meat and hides, stone axes, flint knives and arrowheads to the Pueblos for cotton cloth, corn, beans, squash and Pueblo pottery. Some Navajo bands decided to move nearer to Pueblo villages so they wouldn't have to travel so far to trade. As the years passed, Navajos and Pueblos learned much from one another.

But not all Navajos and Pueblos were friends. Some Navajo bands and Pueblo villages became enemies and carried out raids on each other. When a Navajo band wanted to raid a Pueblo village, the war leader and his men carefully planned their attack. Usually the warriors had to walk many days to reach the enemy village. Once they came near the village, the Navajo men hid themselves and carefully observed the Pueblo people. They noticed when the villagers went to get water, when they went to work in the corn fields, and when groups of Pueblo men left to go hunting. At the right time, the Navajo raiding party moved as close to the village as they could without being seen. Then, suddenly, they'd strike. Their tactic was to surprise and frighten the Pueblo people. While the confused villagers ran for cover and gathered their weapons, the Navajo raiders made their escape. They had to be quick! Soon the Pueblo warriors would be after them!

In those days, Navajos probably took very few Pueblo people prisoners. When they did, many of the prisoners became slaves and had to work for Navajo families. Often they became part of the family. In fact, Navajo men might take captured Pueblo women for wives. When their Pueblo wives had children, they belonged to their Pueblo mother's clan as well as to their Navajo father's clan. In this way, Pueblo women started new Navajo clans.

After a time, the Pueblo prisoners changed the culture of the Navajo bands. Some scientists think that Navajos were aleady farming by this time, but other scientists believe that Navajo people learned how to farm from their Pueblo prisoners. They learned how to plant, care for, harvest, store and grind the corn and they discovered different ways to cook corn, beans and squash. In a few years, many farms grew below the canyon walls of Dinétah. For the first time, Navajo families depended on crops of corn, squash and beans from their farms. They didn't have to depend as much on gathering plants from the land, so they didn't have to travel so often. There was more time to spend around the home, so Navajo families built stronger hogans. They were able to make and own more things. When they did travel, they knew their homes and farms would be waiting for them when they returned.

MAP 3: New Mexico pueblos.

"Pueblo de Taos, New Mexico" by W. H. Jackson, COURTESY OF THE COLORADO HISTORICAL SOCIETY, #WHJ-8213

A CHANGING TRIBE

When Navajos first arrived at Dinétah, they lived much like other Athapaskan people. For hundreds of years, Navajos had lived in hunting and gathering bands and knew many ways to survive by using the land around them. When they came to Dinétah, Navajos brought everything they needed to live off the land.

By the 1600s the Navajo people had become a tribe fully capable of raising their own food. There were farms of corn, beans and squash. Navajo families had food to last them through the dry summers and harsh winters. They still hunted and gathered food, but they depended more and more on their farms to feed them. Slowly the culture began to change. Navajos spent more time planting and harvesting their crops and they used many new tools such as stone or wood hoes. They made flat baskets to dry their corn crop. Dried corn was stored in pots and hidden safely underground or in small caves until needed. Navajo women used grinding stones to grind the dried corn into cornmeal. They baked corn cakes in an earth pit, boiled dried corn in a stew and cooked cornmeal mush on a flat griddle stone heated over a fire.

The first Navajo farmers also learned special prayers to bless their farms. They followed special rules, called taboos, to help the corn grow. Medicine men used corn pollen to bless their farms, their families, their homes and property. The Navajo medicine men used new ceremonies to heal the sick and keep their people healthy.

Farming changed Navajo culture in many ways, but many aspects of hunting and gathering way of life remained. The people still used sinew-backed bows, brown pottery and piñon pitch baskets and they employed old ceremonies for hunting, and curing the sick. Many of these things can still be seen today.

As more and more Navajo bands began farming, their population increased. The farms provided more food and people were healthier. More young children and older band members survived the hard winters. Soon the canyon farm lands were crowded and some bands had to move away to find new places to live and farm. Some migrated westward into Arizona, while others headed south to Mount Taylor in New Mexico, or northward into

"Sacred Mountains of the Navajo," [top left:: Sisnaajinii, top right: Tsoodził, bottom left: Dook'o'ọslííd, bottom right: Dibé Nitsaa']. *Photographs by author, courtesy of the Navajo Nation*

THE SACRED MOUNTAINS

NAVAJO NAME	ENGLISH NAME	SACRED COLOR	DIRECTION
Sisnaajinii	Mount Blanca	White	East
Tsoodził	Mount Taylor	Blue	South
Dook'o'ọslííd	San Francisco Peaks	Yellow	West
Dibé Nitsaa'	Mount Hesperus	Black	North

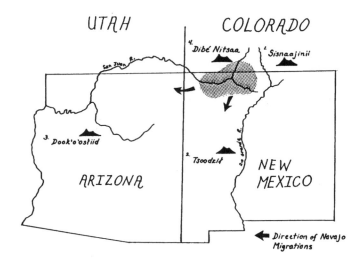

MAP 4: The growth of Navajo Land and
the Four Sacred Mountains

Colorado and Utah.

There was another reason Navajo bands moved. Ute and
other Indian bands were migrating into northern New Mexico.
They needed to use the land, too, so they probably fought with the
Navajo bands who still lived in Dinétah. It was easy for enemies to
find and attack Navajo families. They simply looked for Navajo
hogans and corn fields. Before long, living in Dinétah was too
dangerous for some Navajo families, so they moved to a safer spot.

By the year 1700, Navajos were living in northern Arizona,
New Mexico and probably southern Colorado and Utah, as well.
The Navajo people thought of all this land as Navajo country and
traditional Navajos say that there are four sacred mountains that
mark its boundaries. They say that when the first Navajos came
into this world, the sacred beings First Man and First Woman
made the mountains, dressed them in four colors and put them at
the edges of Navajo land. First Woman gave all the land between
these mountains to the Navajo people. She warned them not to live
outside their sacred land. For this reason, the four sacred mountains are very important to Navajo people. To the east in Colorado
is Sisnaajinii, Mount Blanca. To the south in New Mexico stands
Tsoodził, or Mount Taylor. In the west, near Flagstaff, Arizona, is
Dook'o'ǫsłííd, or the San Francisco Peaks. The northern sacred
mountain, called Dibé Ntsaa, or Mount Hesperus, stands near
Cortez, Colorado.

THE SPANIARDS

Almost five hundred years ago, Navajos began hearing stories from their Pueblo neighbors about the strange men they had seen. These men had thick beards and were dressed in metal helmets and armor. They rode from one place to another on animals that looked like large dogs. As they rode, their iron weapons rattled noisily and the sunlight glinted off their armor. Like a lost war party, they clanked and clanged their way across the American Southwest, stirring up great clouds of dust.

The Navajos named them Naakaii, or Those-Who-Wander-Around. They were the Spaniards. No one knew it then, but the Navajo, Pueblos and Spaniards would change one another's way of life forever.

The Spanish influence started around the year 1492, when Christopher Columbus sailed across the Atlantic Ocean for the king and queen of Spain. Spain was becoming a major power in Europe. For many years the Spaniards had been fighting with their enemies and they needed gold and silver to buy weapons and pay their soldiers. The king and queen also wanted to make Spain rich and powerful.

Columbus was a sea captain and an explorer and, like many other explorers, he believed the world was round. He told the Spanish king and queen that he could bring them the desired riches from Asia by sailing west across the Atlantic Ocean, instead of traveling eastward as others had. He thought it would be a faster way to reach Asia. The king and queen finally agreed with Columbus and they gave him three ships and a crew to make his long voyage across the Atlantic Ocean.

For months Columbus' ships sailed across the unknown waters of the Atlantic. Finally one of his sailors spotted some islands. Columbus was sure he'd reached the East Indies Islands in Asia. He was so sure, he called the people he found living there "Indians." Columbus didn't know it then,

MAP 5: Columbus and other Spanish explorers sailed to the New World from Spain by crossing the Atlantic Ocean.

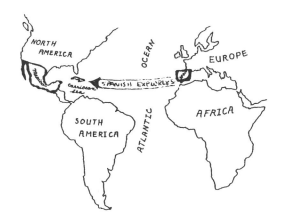

"Chiefs announce to Montezuma the arrival of the Spaniards," COURTESY OF THE SPECIAL COLLECTIONS LIBRARY, NORTHERN ARIZONA UNIVERSITY, JOHNSTON COLLECTION, #NAU-413-1283

"Cortez," from slide by Johnston, COURTESY OF THE SPECIAL COLLECTIONS LIBRARY, NORTHERN ARIZONA UNIVERSITY, JOHNSTON COLLECTION, #NAU-413

but he had actually reached America! In 1492, people in Europe had no idea North and South America existed. Although Columbus had failed to reach Asia, the Spaniards still felt he had made a great discovery. They named North and South America "The New World," but it wasn't really new at all. The American Indians had already been living there for thousands of years.

Stories of the New World traveled back to Spain and many Spaniards dreamed of becoming rich in America. They sailed across the Atlantic and settled the islands Columbus had found. Some Spaniards lived and traded with the Indians there. Others fought the Indians or made them into slaves. By 1510, Spanish towns and farms dotted the islands.

In 1519, Hernando Cortez learned there was a great Indian tribe living in Mexico called the Aztecs. Aztec kings and princes dressed in gold jewelry and beautiful feathers and lived in great cities of stone. Stories about the Aztecs excited Cortez, so he bought weapons, raised an army and sailed to Mexico. Once his army landed there, Cortez discovered that the Aztecs had a huge army and were very powerful. Proud, brave, and fierce warriors, they had conquered many Mexican Indian tribes. As strong as they were, they had never fought against men with horses, guns and cannons and they didn't realize Cortez was planning to conquer them. Many Aztec leaders believed the Spaniards were messengers from the Aztec gods.

Cortez hoped to take the Aztec's gold and land for himself, his men and the king and queen of Spain. He knew his small army would need help to conquer the Aztec nation. Cortez learned that many Mexican Indian tribes hated the Aztecs because the Aztecs had been cruel to these tribes. When they learned Cortez wanted to defeat the Aztecs, thousands of Indian warriors joined the small Spanish army. Together, they attacked the mighty Aztec nation and, after two years of bloody fighting, Cortez's Spanish and Indian army conquered the Aztecs. Cortez took the Aztec leaders as prisoner. The Spaniards renamed Mexico "New Spain" and forced the Aztec people to serve the king of Spain. The Spaniards ordered them to build new cities and churches and they demanded that the Indians work for them on farms and ranches.

Spanish soldiers then began to explore all of Mexico. They conquered many Indian tribes and as the years passed, Spanish towns and ranches grew. Indian slaves worked in Spanish gold and silver mines. The Spaniards shipped the gold and silver to Spain and before long these riches made Spain a very powerful nation.

The Spaniards living in New Spain then began to consider that there might be more rich Indian cities waiting to be conquered.

One story claimed that far to the north there were seven cities made of gold, called the Seven Cities of Cíbola. If only someone could find them! A Spanish explorer named Francisco Coronado decided to try. He raised an army and, in 1540, he and his men headed northward.

After a long and difficult journey, Coronado and his army entered the territory now called New Mexico. They didn't find the gold cities, but they did find the Zuni pueblo of Hawaikúh. The Spaniards were disappointed. Still Coronado hoped the Zunis could feed his hungry army. Perhaps they could tell him where to find gold and silver. Coronado ordered his men to attack the pueblo and the Zuni warriors fought bravely but they couldn't stop the Spaniards. The loud guns and charging horses terrified them. Their arrows and spears bounced off the Spaniards' armor while Spanish swords and lances cut the Zuni warriors down. Finally the Zunis retreated and left Coronado standing in an empty village.

"Temple of the Sun," COURTESY OF THE SPECIAL COLLECTIONS LIBRARY, NORTHERN ARIZONA UNIVERSITY, JOHNSTON COLLECTION, #NAU-413-1845B

After the battle of Hawaikúh Coronado sent groups of soldiers out to explore the land. The news of Coronado's attack spread through New Mexico. Many Pueblo Indians realized the Spaniards might attack them next. They decided on a plan to save their villages. When the Spanish soldiers arrived at the each village, the Pueblos told them that there were rich lands to the east. They were very far away but, the Pueblo chiefs promised, if the soldiers would just keep riding, they would find much gold. The news excited Coronado and, anxiously, he led his army eastward out of New Mexico. The Pueblos hoped they would never see the soldiers again. They knew Coronado might spend years searching for riches, but he'd never find them.

"The Battle of Hawaikúh," from John Twitchell, *The Leading Facts of New Mexican History*, Torch Press, 1911-1917

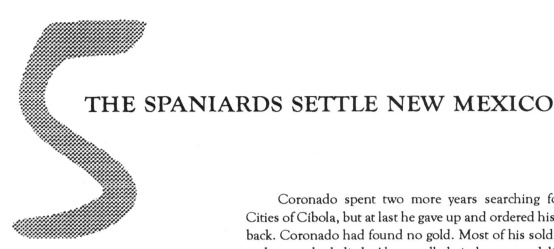THE SPANIARDS SETTLE NEW MEXICO

Coronado spent two more years searching for the Seven Cities of Cíbola, but at last he gave up and ordered his army to turn back. Coronado had found no gold. Most of his soldiers were sick and many had died. Almost all their horses and livestock were gone. As the Spaniards struggled along, they threw away much of their heavy armor and weapons. All they wanted was to go home to Mexico.

On the way back, when Coronado's army reached the Rio Grande Valley in New Mexico, the Pueblos were waiting. They hadn't forgotten about how Coronado and his men had treated them. As the Spaniards marched southward, Pueblo warriors raided and ambushed them. Finally Coronado's army left New Mexico.

After Coronado, almost forty years passed before other small parties of Spanish soldiers explored the Southwest. Although they never stayed long, the Spaniards were actually planning to settle the Rio Grande Valley. In 1598, a huge Spanish army marched into New Mexico. These Spaniards brought weapons and armor, but they also brought tools to build homes and start farms. Oxen

MAP 6: Oñate in New Mexico

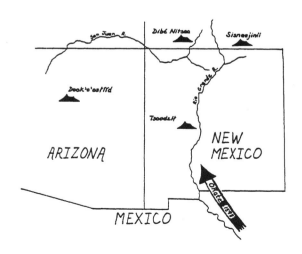

pulled clumsy wagons loaded with hammers and saws, shovels, hoes, lanterns, chairs, bundles of cloth and sacks full of seed. The soldiers' families bumped along in the rumbling ox carts while great herds of sheep, goats and cattle stirred up clouds of dust.

The leader of the army was Juan de Oñate. Although Oñate hoped to find gold and silver, he was mainly looking for good farm and ranch lands. He wanted to start a colony, or town, on the banks of the Rio Grande River. He also planned to bring the Spanish religion and culture to the Pueblo people. Oñate, his priests and

"Inscription by Juan de Oñate" at El Morro National Monument, photograph by author, COURTESY NATIONAL PARKS ADMINISTRATION [The inscription reads, "*Passed by here the Governor Don Juan de Oñate from the discovery of the Sea of the south on the 16th day of April, 1605.*"]

his Spanish colonists had come to settle New Mexico.

But the Pueblo Indians did not want the Spaniards in their lands and they were not interested in learning the Spanish way of life. They wanted to fight against the soldiers but Oñate's army was powerful. As the Spanish army marched northward, Oñate stopped at each Pueblo. He met with the village leaders and told them that his people were settling New Mexico for the king of Spain. He expected the Indians to help them. Most Pueblo leaders decided to agree with Oñate while they hoped that he, his settlers and his soldiers would soon leave New Mexico, just as Coronado's army had done.

Oñate wanted the Pueblos to help support his people so he demanded that some of the Pueblo Indians give up their homes and crops to his soldiers. Spaniards forced other Pueblo people to build adobe homes for them and at times soldiers just took whatever they wanted from the villagers. The Spanish priests believed they could help the Indians by teaching them about God. The priests wanted the Pueblos to stop holding their traditional ceremonies and believing in their own religions. Although some priests and

[above, left] "New Mexico-Acoma-The Mesa," photograph by W. H. Jackson, COURTESY OF THE COLORADO HISTORICAL SOCIETY, #WHJ-32779

[above, right] "Mesa Encantada, New Mexico, showing Acoma Pueblo" photograph by W. H. Jackson, COURTESY OF THE COLORADO HISTORICAL SOCIETY, #WHJ-11303

soldiers treated Pueblo people kindly, others did not. They destroyed sacred Pueblo masks and prayer sticks and arrested, whipped or killed any Pueblo medicine man they caught holding a traditional ceremony. Spanish soldiers forced Pueblos to build mission churches in their villages where the priests could teach them about the Spanish god. Many Pueblo people had to work as mission cooks and maids, sheepherders and gardeners. They had less time to work on their own farms and support their own families. But the Pueblo people had no choice because the soldiers punished anyone who refused to follow the priests' orders. If Pueblo people attacked the priests and soldiers, Oñate sent his army to punish them. Many villagers were killed or wounded. Often the Pueblo survivors were taken away to be sold as slaves.

Acoma Pueblo, like other Pueblos, had agreed to Oñate's demand that the Indians help the Spaniards. Still, if the Spaniards made excessive demands, the Acomas were willing to fight them.

One day an Indian messenger stumbled into Acoma with bad news. A group of Oñate's soldiers were riding toward the village! The Acoma chiefs discussed what they should do. Acoma was far from the Rio Grande Valley and the Spanish army and stood on a high, steep-sided mesa. There was only one narrow trail leading to the top and the tall mesa cliffs were nearly impossible to climb. Acoma warriors could be fierce fighters and there was also a group of Mount Taylor Navajos visiting Acoma. The chiefs felt their village would be safe from any attack but, just in case a fight started, they asked the visiting Navajos to help them.

But only nineteen soldiers arrived! The Acoma chiefs allowed the Spaniards to come up the trail and into their village. They had come to collect Acoma property for Oñate and his colonists. The Spanish captain ordered the villagers to bring them the supplies. Suddenly an argument started and Acoma warriors rushed at the surprised soldiers, killing the captain and thirteen of his men. Five soldiers escaped by dashing back down the village trail or jumping off the tall mesa into the sand dunes far below.

When the survivors told Oñate about the battle, he ordered seventy soldiers to ride back and destroy Acoma. But the Acomas and their Navajo friends were ready. The chiefs set guards at the top of the village trail, and when the Spaniards started to ascend, Acoma warriors shot arrows and hurled stones down on the soldiers' heads. The Spaniards had to retreat. For two days Oñate's men tried to fight their way up the trail, but each time they were beaten back. When the soldiers rested, they could hear the warriors calling them names and laughing from the mesa top.

The battle at Acoma Pueblo.

The Spaniards realized they could never force their way up the village trail, so they devised another plan. Secretly they sent soldiers with bundles of ropes to the far side of Acoma mesa. Carefully, they climbed the dangerously tall, steep mesa cliffs. When the soldiers finally reached the top, they lowered their ropes back down the cliffs and used them to haul up heavy cannons. The soldiers set the cannons up at the mesa's edge and aimed them at the village.

Without warning, loud explosions echoed across Acoma mesa. Cannon balls whistled overhead and crashed into the village, smashing roof beams and shattering adobe walls. The surprised Acoma warriors scattered, leaving the village trail unguarded. This was the chance the Spaniards below had been waiting for. With a shout, they rushed up the empty trail and swept into Acoma village. In the confusion the soldiers killed many Acomas. To save themselves, many people had to leap off the cliffs into the sand dunes far below.

The fight for Acoma was over. Oñate's men had captured the village and over five hundred Acoma prisoners. The soldiers completely destroyed the village and punished each Acoma man taken prisoner by cutting off one foot and forcing him to work for twenty years serving the settlers. Acoma women were also forced to serve the settlers for twenty years. All the captured Acoma children were sent away to be raised in Spanish missions. Oñate hoped that other Pueblos would see how he had punished Acoma, so they would be afraid to fight.

The Navajos who survived the battle told their people about the fight at Acoma. It was clear that Oñate's soldiers could be a dangerous enemy.

6 THE HORSE

After conquering the Pueblos, Spanish colonists founded small towns along the Rio Grande River. Santa Fe was founded in 1610 and became the most important town in the New Mexican colony. The Spanish governor and other Spanish leaders lived in Santa Fe. Many colonists settled near Pueblo villages while the mission priests and soldiers lived in the villages. The Spanish soldiers living at the pueblo protected the priest and made sure the villagers followed his orders.

Navajo people were not as threatened by the Spaniards as were the Pueblos. Their land was far from the Spanish towns and Spanish soldiers. Navajo people were still free to live their own way of life. Yet many Navajos became interested in getting some of the things the colonists had. Axes, knives and pots were made of iron. They were strong and lasted a long time. Spanish cotton and wool cloth made good blankets and clothing. As they had with the Pueblos, some Navajo bands began trading with the Spanish colonists. Other bands raided the colonists to get the things they wanted. At times, Navajo warriors brought back captured livestock

"Mexican house, near Santa Fe, New Mexico, ca. 1865," photographer unknown, COURTESY OF THE MUSEUM OF NEW MEXICO, #10632

"Early Navajo Horsemen, Indians, Navajo, Biography (men, unidentified)" photographer unknown, COURTESY OF THE DENVER PUBLIC LIBRARY, WESTERN HISTORY DEPARTMENT, F#20039

from Spanish farms and ranches. In those days, Navajos didn't raise livestock. Captured sheep, goats, and cattle were butchered and eaten right away.

Of all the things the Navajo people got from the Spaniards, horses became the most valuable. Before Navajos were able to ride horses, warriors had to travel and fight on foot. The Spanish soldiers fought on horseback. The Navajo men knew that a Spanish horseman could ride down and kill the fastest runner. When they went raiding, Navajo warriors had to depend on careful plans and surprise attacks to survive. But by the early 1600s, Navajos had learned to ride horses. They began raiding the Spaniards and other enemies on horseback. Soon Navajo warriors had become better horsemen than the Spanish soldiers!

The horse had changed the way Navajos fought their enemies. On horses, warriors could travel rapidly over long distances. Navajo raiders were quicker in battle, too. On horseback, a warrior wore only a few clothes so he could move freely. He took off his heavy buckskin shirt and leggings. Navajo men carried light weapons. The bow and arrow, shield and spear were easier to use than heavy Spanish guns and swords. The warrior rode bareback and used a rawhide rope for reins. Not many Spaniards could stop a swift Navajo raiding party when they swept down onto a ranch. By the time the Spaniards got their guns and horses, the Navajo warriors had galloped away with the rancher's livestock. Spanish horses had to carry all the soldiers' heavy armor and weapons. They were too loaded down to catch the quick Navajo war ponies.

Navajo people took great pride in being excellent horsemen. Young boys learned all the riding skills they would need to be good hunters and fighters. Navajo raiders became a threat to Spanish settlements and few colonists dared to move onto Navajo land. In

On horses people were able
to travel rapidly over long distances.

this way, the horse helped the Navajos stop Spaniards from settling in Navajo territory.

Horses also helped Navajos travel great distances to hunt and trade. These strong animals brought back bundles of Pueblo and Spanish trade goods. Navajo families could own more things because horses could carry them all. Many families collected buffalo robes, trade blankets, axes, knives, silver jewelry, bridles and bits. They began keeping large herds.

Bands that had many horses became richer than bands that had only a few. Leaders of rich Navajo bands became important headmen. The headmen shared their riches with their family and relatives so people respected and listened to them. At times, smaller bands decided to join a rich headman's band. They depended on the wealthy headman to help and protect them. They followed his advice. In this way, some Navajo bands became larger, stronger and more important than other bands.

Horses also allowed headmen from different bands to visit one another more easily. They met to trade and attend ceremonies. They discussed their hopes, worries, troubles and plans. Often the headmen agreed to help one another fight their enemies.

The horse also made Navajo territory grow. Navajos who had horses were able to use the land better. They could live farther from wood and water. They could live farther from their farms. Horses could take people into the canyons and onto mesas faster than by just walking. Horses could carry more water bags, bundles of firewood, and sacks of corn than a person could. Navajos were able to live farther from their relatives' homes, too. Often they were forced to live farther away. Horse herds needed plenty of grazing land. The more horses a family owned, the more grazing land their herd needed. As the years passed, Navajo land grew. Little by little, the Navajo people filled up the land between the four sacred mountains and the horse became a sacred Navajo animal.

THE PUEBLO REBELLION

Life for the Pueblo Indians during the 1600s was hard. The Spaniards had settled on their lands and Spanish towns and ranches dotted the Rio Grande Valley. Soldiers and priests were living in the Pueblo villages. The Spanish priests outlawed traditional Pueblo ceremonies and forced the Indians to worship the Spanish god. If any Indian refused, he was beaten, jailed or killed. The Pueblos knew that if they tried to fight against the Spaniards at the mission, soldiers from Santa Fe might come and destroy their village.

Strange diseases brought by the settlers from Europe also swept through many Pueblo towns. The illnesses killed hundreds of people and left many villages empty. Before Oñate and his colonists had come, the Pueblos had always prepared for dry times by storing extra food for their villages. Even if rain didn't fall and their farms died, the people would have food. When the Spaniards conquered the Pueblos, they forced them to surrender the stored food as taxes. When dry times came, there was no food and hundreds of Pueblo people died from starvation. The people began to abandon their villages to get away from diseases, hunger and the Spaniards. Some joined their Navajo friends living near Dinétah. Others joined the Zunis or the Hopis, far to the west. Some Pueblos even moved out onto the plains to escape. When Oñate first entered New Mexico in 1598, there were over one hundred Pueblo Indian villages in the Rio Grande Valley. By 1680, only forty-three were left.

By 1680, many Pueblo chiefs had decided something had to be done about the Spaniards. The Pueblo way of life was dying. A San Juan Pueblo leader named Popé held a secret meeting with other Pueblo leaders. He knew that if a single Pueblo village fought against the Spaniards, the army could easily destroy it. But what could the Spanish army do if all Pueblos attacked the Spaniards at the same time? There would be too many villages to fight.

Popé outlined his plan to the chiefs and chose a day in August of 1680 for the rebellion. On that day, Pueblo warriors from all villages would storm into the churches and kill all the priests and

"Taos Pueblo, 1880," photograph by John K. Hillers, COURTESY OF THE MUSEUM OF NEW MEXICO. #16096

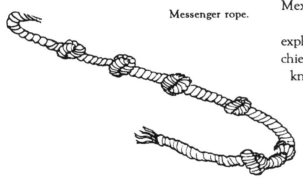

Messenger rope.

soldiers. Not one Spaniard should escape to warn the governor and soldiers in Santa Fe. When the priests and their soldiers were dead, the warriors would join together to form a huge Pueblo Indian army, march into Santa Fe, and drive the Spaniards out of New Mexico.

But how would the villages know just when to attack? Popé explained that each day he would send messengers to each village chief. Each messenger would carry a knotted rope. The number of knots on the rope told how many days were left. Each day the village chief received the rope, he would untie one knot. If seven knots were left, that meant there would be seven days left. When all the knots had been untied, the Pueblos would attack. The chiefs agreed with Popé's plan and they returned to their villages to get ready. Popé left for the northern pueblo of Taos where he could direct the rebellion in secret.

At first, Popé's plan went well. Then, four days before the rebellion, he discovered that someone had informed the Spaniards about it. Popé knew the Pueblos had to strike quickly, before the soldiers could attack them. He immediately sent messengers dashing to each village. Attack the Spaniards!

So on August 9th, 1680, the Pueblos rebelled. Pueblo warriors killed every priest and soldier they could find and then joined together in a huge army and marched towards Santa Fe. The surviving Spanish colonists retreated into Santa Fe for safety but the governor, Antonio de Otermín, knew he couldn't protect the settlers. The Pueblo army surrounded Santa Fe and cut off all supplies to the town. After a week Otermín knew his people couldn't survive much longer. He ordered his soldiers and colonists to abandon Santa Fe. The governor and nearly two thousand Span-

"Mission, Laguna Pueblo, ca. 1910," photographer unknown, COURTESY OF THE MUSEUM OF NEW MEXICO. #66639

iards fled to friendly Isleta Pueblo for protection, then marched down the Rio Grande Valley towards Mexico. At last they reached the Spanish settlement at El Paso in what is now known as Texas.

The Spaniards had escaped, but they had lost the war and over three hundred Spanish colonists had been killed. They had lost their homes, ranches, missions and most of their belongings. Not one Spaniard was left in New Mexico. Popé's Pueblo rebellion had worked. The Pueblos celebrated and tore down Spanish buildings and burned the churches. They destroyed much of Santa Fe. The Pueblo Indians were sure the Spaniards would never come back.

Ten years passed. The Pueblo warriors returned to their villages and to their traditional way of life. Medicine men resumed their traditional ceremonies without fear. Pueblo villages began trading freely with each other again, as well as with Navajo bands, just as they had before the Spaniards.

Yet the Pueblos had many problems. Navajos raided Pueblo villages as they had before, but there were no Spanish soldiers to protect them. Mounted on swift ponies, Navajo attacks on their Pueblo enemies increased. Apache and Ute horseman raided the Pueblos as well. Some Pueblo villages even fought with each other. During this time, the Spaniards made three tries at reconquering the Rio Grande Valley, but failed. Many Pueblo villages were so busy fighting among themselves and with their traditional enemies that they hardly noticed the Spanish soldiers come and go!

But Spanish leaders in Mexico hadn't forgotten the Pueblos or New Mexico. Undaunted, they chose a new Spaniard, Don

"Down the Arroyo to Santa
Fe, N.M." from painting, Frank Reeve
Collection, COURTESY OF THE SPECIAL
COLLECTIONS DEPARTMENT, GENERAL
LIBRARY, UNIVERSITY OF NEW MEXICO,
#000-158-0092

Diego de Vargas, to be governor. Vargas was to go to El Paso, form an army, and reconquer New Mexico for Spain.

Vargas arrived in El Paso in 1691 and immediately made plans to invade the Rio Grande Valley. He learned from spies that Popé's army had fallen apart. He also knew the Pueblos were fighting with their enemies and among themselves. Vargas spent a year preparing his army. In 1692, Vargas and his men marched out of El Paso, into New Mexico and caught most of the villages by surprise. Soon Governor Vargas' men had taken Santa Fe and, one by one, his army defeated the Pueblo villages. Although Popé had already died, soldiers caught and killed other leaders of the Pueblo rebellion. Most Pueblo people surrendered, but many ran away. After four years of war, Vargas and his men had reconquered all of the Pueblos. The Spaniards were back and they were back to stay.

"Don José Diego de Vargas Zapata y
Luján (1643-1704)," from painting,
COURTESY OF THE MUSEUM OF
NEW MEXICO. #11409

LEARNING NEW WAYS

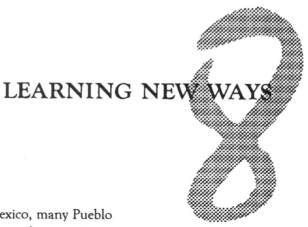

After the Spaniards reconquered New Mexico, many Pueblo people abandoned their villages to escape Vargas' army. Some northern Pueblos fled to Dinétah to live with friendly Navajo bands where they hoped to be safe from the soldiers. The Navajos in Dinétah welcomed them. These homeless Pueblos had been their friends and trading partners.

The Pueblos who joined the Dinétah Navajos brought many things from their own culture. While they lived together, Navajos and Pueblos learned much about each other's way of life. They shared hunting, gathering and farming skills. They learned one another's arts and crafts. Navajo and Pueblo medicine men exchanged prayers, ceremonies and legends. Many scientists believe that much of traditional Navajo religion and legend came from the Pueblo people living in Dinétah. They believe that Navajos adopted important ideas, such as sand painting and Yeiibicheii masks, from the Pueblos. Navajo medicine men realized that their people could use some of these things. As the years passed, Navajos took many Pueblo ideas and adapted them to Navajo culture.

The Pueblos who fled to Dinétah brought many things from Spanish culture, as well. While at the missions, they had learned to use Spanish tools and raise livestock. When the Pueblos came to Dinétah, they drove flocks of sheep and goats ahead of them and carried bundles of Spanish goods on their backs.

The Navajos in Dinétah soon learned to raise livestock. They discovered that they didn't have to depend solely on hunting to get meat. All they had to do was butcher a sheep or goat. They learned to shear the sheep for wool and to spin the wool into yarn. Navajo women began using different plants to dye the yarn. They built looms to weave the colored yarn into clothing, just as their Pueblo neighbors did. Navajo women wove blankets, dresses, ponchos and belts from wool yarn. People found that wool clothing lasted a long time and it was comfortable and good-looking.

It wasn't long before raising livestock became an important

[above] "Navajo woman in traditional dress," photographer unknown, COURTESY OF THE ARIZONA HISTORICAL SOCIETY, PIONEER MUSEUM IN THE SPECIAL COLLECTIONS LIBRARY, NORTHERN ARIZONA UNIVERSITY, #NAHPS-666-743

FACING PAGE:
[top] "Bringing down the batten," from an American Bureau of Ethnology engraving, COURTESY OF THE MUSEUM OF NEW MEXICO HISTORY LIBRARY.

[middle] "Navajo woman weaving a belt," from an American Bureau of Ethnology engraving, COURTESY OF THE MUSEUM OF NEW MEXICO HISTORY LIBRARY.

[bottom] "Navajo woman spinning," from an American Bureau of Ethnology engraving, COURTESY OF THE MUSEUM OF NEW MEXICO HISTORY LIBRARY.

part of Navajo culture. Sheep and goats gave people enough to eat all year around. Caring for the livestock took up much of a Navajo family's time. The women and their children usually watched over the flocks. Most of the sheep became property of the women, so sheep made Navajo women more important, too.

Soon the skills of raising livestock spread among all the Navajo people. Many families became rich with thousands of sheep and goats. Poorer families struggled to get livestock and they would trade with other families to get some, or join bands that had many sheep. Young men often hoped to marry women who had large flocks. Many times the quickest and easiest way to start a flock or make it bigger was to raid Spanish and Pueblo settlements along the Rio Grande.

Meanwhile, the Spaniards had conquered the Pueblos, but they had trouble keeping the peace. Some Pueblos were still fighting the Spaniards. To make things worse, Navajo, Apache, and Ute raids threatened Spanish settlements. The Spaniards feared the fighting would destroy the Spanish way of life in New Mexico. Spanish leaders realized they couldn't fight the Pueblos and the Navajos, Apaches, and Utes all at once. Somehow, they had to make peace with some of their enemies. The Spanish governor offered to make alliances with the Pueblos and other tribes of the American Southwest. If the Pueblos would keep the peace, the Spaniards would help them fight their enemies.

Vargas' reconquest of New Mexico had terribly weakened the Pueblos. Each year there were less Pueblo people and more Hispanic New Mexicans. The Pueblos realized the Spaniards would never again leave New Mexico. They also knew they needed help fighting their enemies so the Pueblo people had little choice. They agreed to cooperate with the priests, soldiers and Spanish leaders. Yet, secretly, the Pueblos held their traditional ceremonies and followed their traditional way of life.

As the years passed, the Spaniards treated the Pueblos more kindly. Soldiers and Hispanic settlers respected Pueblo homes and belongings and Spanish leaders respected Pueblo village chiefs. Priests no longer arrested or beat Pueblo medicine men. They were not allowed to destroy sacred Pueblo masks and belongings. Many Pueblo people began to feel they could live with the Spaniards after all. As the news spread, Pueblo families began returning to their abandoned villages. Many of the Pueblo Indians living in Dinétah left their Navajo friends and moved back to their homes.

But the Navajo had no wish to live with the Spaniards. They didn't want to have anything to do with priests, churches or Spanish religion. Navajo families wanted to be free to move their sheep herds from one grazing spot to another. Some Navajos traded with the Hispanic settlers, but others continued raiding New Mexican settlements for livestock. Navajo warriors, as well as Apaches and Utes, also raided Pueblo villages. The Spaniards offered to help defend the Pueblo villages from Navajo raids. In return, they hoped the Pueblos would join Spanish military expeditions against the Navajos. The Pueblos began depending on the Spaniards to protect them. Many Pueblo warriors helped the soldiers by guiding military expeditions through Navajo land and planning attacks on Navajo settlements. Hispanic and Pueblo raiders destroyed Navajo homes, killed or captured the livestock and took Navajo women and children for slaves.

By 1720, Navajos were raiding most Pueblo and Hispanic settlements. They were also fighting traditional enemies such as the Comanches and the Utes. Then came a time of peace. Between 1720 and 1773, the Navajos, Spaniards and Pueblos ended their fighting. Navajo and Spanish leaders worked together to keep the peace. Navajo were free to travel and trade in safety and without the threat of enemy raids, Navajo families, farms and livestock grew.

In 1773, the Comanches attacked the Navajos. The Navajo headmen blamed the Spaniards for the attack because they knew the Spaniards and Comanches were allies. They believed the Spanish governor had encouraged the Comanches to attack them. Times of peace were over. Navajo raiders struck New Mexican settlements. The Spaniards and their allies struck back. Ute, Comanche, Jicarilla and Mescalero Apache warriors raided Navajo homes. The war became so threatening that Navajos living in Dinétah had to build their homes behind stone walls on top of steep cliffs. People moved away. After years of war, almost all the Navajo people had abandoned Dinétah. It was too dangerous.

The Navajos searched for safer lands. Navajo families migrated to the south and west, driving their flocks of sheep ahead of them. Their herds roamed the grassy meadows around Ramah, near Zuni. They grazed in the Chuska Mountains, on Black Mesa, and along the Little Colorado River. Navajo stock wandered the northern slopes of Dook'o'oslííd in Arizona. People drove their animals across the San Juan River and into the canyons of Utah. Wherever there was safe grazing land, Navajo families made their homes.

Despite the threat of enemy raids, the Navajo people had become one of the largest and richest people in the Southwest. Herds of Navajo horses, sheep, goats and cattle covered the land. Navajo farms dotted the canyons. Navajo warriors were skilled raiders and continued capturing livestock and slaves. Yet life was

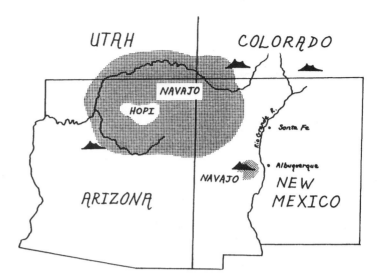

MAP 7: In times of peace and war,
Navajo territory grew rapidly during
the 1700s.

more perilous than ever. The Navajo people had many enemies and
each year many Navajos were killed or captured by raiding parties.
These raiders earned money selling their Navajo prisoners in Santa
Fe, then bought guns to use against other Navajos. At times, armies
of Spanish soldiers and ranchers invaded Navajo country and
people had to flee for their lives. They often returned to find their
homes and all their belongings destroyed.

In those dangerous times, the Navajo people need good
leaders to protect them. Navajo leaders had to be thoughtful, careful
and wise. One of the most famous was a man from the Chuska
Mountains of Arizona. His name was Naabaahii, the Raider. The
Spaniards called him Narbona.

NARBONA

Narbona was born in 1766, somewhere in the Chuska Mountains of Arizona. He belonged to the Táchii'nii, or Red Streaked Earth Clan. No one remembers his boyhood name, but years later people called him Naabaahii, or the Raider. It was a dangerous time for children to grow up. No one knew when Comanche, Ute, New Mexican, or Spanish raiders would attack their home. Like most small children, little Narbona stayed near his mother. When enemies attacked, she snatched him up and hid in the mountains. The family stayed there until the Navajo men chased the raiders away. Narbona learned about danger early in his life. He had heard the war cries, seen the flash of guns and smelled the smoke of burning hogans.

When Narbona was six years old, his father gave the boy his first pony. Narbona spent time riding bareback with the other boys in camp and soon became an excellent rider. He practiced jumping, throwing stones and tossing the rabbit stick to make himself strong. Each morning his father made him run. Even if snow lay deep around the hogan and the cold stung his feet, he ran, dressed in only a loincloth. If he was lazy, his father scolded him.

"Run! Roll in the snow! You can stand the cold! Make yourself tough so little things can't kill you off!"

Narbona learned well and it was a good thing he did. When he was just seven, Utes began raiding Chuska Navajo homes. Often the boy and his family had to run for their lives, chasing their sheep into the safety of a canyon. Many times Narbona cut his feet and scraped his legs on sharp rocks. No matter how sore and tired he felt, he never cried or complained. He knew that if he did, the Utes might hear him and discover his family's hiding place.

Through the passing winters, the tough little boy grew tall. One day when Narbona was twelve, his father gave him his first set of bow and arrows, wrapped in a quiver of mountain lion fur. At last he had become a man! Soon he would go on his first raid against his people's enemies.

"Narbona," from drawing by R. H. Kern, COURTESY OF THE MUSEUM OF NEW MEXICO HISTORY LIBRARY.

Cubero, old Mexican Village, at the foot of Mt Taylor (old San Mateo)

[above] "Cubero, old Mexican village at the foot of Mt. Taylor (old San Mateo), ca. 1890," photograph by Ben Wittick, COURTESY OF THE SCHOOL OF AMERICAN RESEARCH COLLECTIONS IN THE MUSEUM OF NEW MEXICO, #15758

By the time he was fifteen, Narbona was a skilled warrior. He charged the enemy, dodging their bullets and arrows and he always returned home safely, driving captured livestock and prisoners into his family's camp. When it was time for Narbona to marry, his relatives found him a wife. Her name was Bikee' Dijool, or Round Footed Girl. She was from a well-known family and her father was an important Chuska headman. Some time after he married Bikee' Dijool, Narbona captured and married a Zuni woman. Later he took Bikee' Dijool's sister for his third wife. The years passed and Narbona grew rich in livestock, slaves, and children.

By 1800, Narbona was a wealthy and famous war leader. He was also thoughtful, generous and caring. People respected him, so when Bikee' Dijool's father passed away the Chuska Navajos chose Narbona to be their new headman. He was only thirty four years old. He had two thousand sheep and goats, fifty head of cattle and over two hundred horses. Narbona was so wealthy he began taking care of the children and the elderly who had lost their families from war. Poor Navajo families asked to join his people and agreed to help care for Narbona's herds. Some small Navajo bands joined Narbona's people for protection from enemies.

One day, Narbona learned that the New Mexicans were settling around Mount Taylor. The governor in Santa Fe was giving sacred Navajo land to the Hispanic ranchers and farmers. This angered many Navajo headmen and several of them complained about the settlers to the Spanish leaders, but nothing changed. The settlers remained on sacred Navajo land. Several Navajo leaders wanted to attack the Spanish settlements, destroy them and drive the settlers off Mount Taylor, but Narbona disagreed. He knew the power of the Spanish army. He knew what war could do to his people. He decided to try talking to the Spaniards once more. In March of 1804, Narbona and a group of headmen made a long, dangerous trip to Santa Fe for a peace meeting with the Spanish governor.

The peace meeting did not go well. Governor Chacón refused to stop giving the land away. Not only that, the governor told the headmen that the Spaniards were going to build a fort near Mount Taylor to protect the settlers. It would be near the Spanish town of Cebolleta. Unhappily, the headmen returned to their homes. Peace had failed, so they decided to fight. Narbona and the other

headmen gathered their warriors and that April, Navajo raiders attacked ranches and farms. The Spaniards and their Ute and Jicarilla allies struck back. They attacked Navajo settlements during the summer of 1804, burning corn fields and homes. Narbona and the other headmen continued to fight. In August, a thousand Navajo warriors raided the town of Cebolleta. Governor Chacón then ordered his soldiers to march deep into Navajo land. It was already winter when the Spanish military expedition entered Canyon de Chelly. The soldiers destroyed every Navajo camp they found, killing the Navajos they met and leaving many families homeless.

By April of 1805, war was taking its toll on both Navajos and Spaniards. Their leaders agreed to meet and sign a treaty of peace. Narbona's war had not driven the settlers away from the sacred mountain, but they had saved some Navajo territory around Mount Taylor. In the treaty, the Spanish leaders had promised to protect Navajo grazing and farming lands surrounding Mount

[above, left] "Mount Taylor, From the Summit of Zuni Pass, Sept. 18," from drawing by R. H. Kern, COURTESY OF THE MUSEUM OF NEW MEXICO LIBRARY.

[above, right] "View of the Cañon of Chelly near its head, five miles southwest of camp 17-September 5th," drawing by R.H. Kern, COURTESY OF THE MUSEUM OF NEW MEXICO HISTORY LIBRARY.

"The wealth of the Navajos, a view in
Arizona, ca. 1890," photograph by Ben
Wittick, COURTESY OF THE MUSEUM OF NEW
MEXICO, # 16465

Taylor. The Spaniards kept their promise. They stopped ranchers
and farmers from settling on Navajo lands and for the next eleven
years, Navajos and Spaniards lived in peace.

But in 1816 war broke out again. After three years of fighting,
the headmen and the Spaniards signed yet another peace treaty.
Narbona hoped that the treaty of 1819 would protect his people
from enemy raids, but the fighting continued. To make things
worse, no rains came to the Chuska Mountains. Streams dried up
and the grass died. The corn plants shriveled under the hot sun and
finally Narbona and his people had to leave their mountain valleys.
They packed their belongings, gathered their livestock and started
westward, searching for grazing lands. As they approached the Hopi
area, they found enough water and grass to keep their animals alive.
The Chuska Navajos settled there at a place called Dinébito'.
Narbona's people and the Hopis became friends and they began
trading with and helping each other. One of Narbona's daughters
and two of his sons married Hopis. But best of all, Narbona was
able to keep his people safe from their enemies.

THE MEXICANS

One day Navajo travelers stopped at Dinébito' to visit with Narbona. They had good news. Rain was falling in the Chuska Mountains! The dry times were over so Narbona's people gathered their livestock and headed back to their mountain homeland. When they reached the Ganado valley just west of the Chuska Mountains, they stopped there to let their stock graze on the tall meadow grass. A group of Navajos rode into Narbona's camp and with them was a young man named Holy Boy. Later he would be known as Hastiin Ch'ilhaajinii, Man of the Black Plants Place. The New Mexicans would call him Manuelito. He belonged to the Bit'ahnii, or Under His Cover Clan, and was a skilled warrior. Manuelito was the son of Cayetano, an important Navajo leader from the Carrizo Mountains north of Canyon de Chelly. Narbona knew Manuelito was full of fight, but he felt the young man would become a leader someday. Manuelito could be a great help to the Chuska Navajos so Narbona arranged a marriage between Manuelito and one of his daughters. After their marriage, Cayetano's people and Narbona's people would be related. Narbona knew, he could count on Cayetano's friendship and help. So when Narbona's band finally left the Ganado valley for home, Manuelito went with them.

At last the Chuska Navajos reached their mountains. Rain clouds drifted over the peaks and green grass covered the mountain valleys. The people set their herds loose to graze and began clearing weeds out of their old farmlands and rebuilding their homes.

But while Narbona's people were living safely at Dinébito' things were happening in Mexico that would change Navajo lives in the years to come.

When Cortez and his men came to the New World in the 1500s, there were over two million Indians living in Mexico. The Spaniards conquered the Indian nations there, but they didn't destroy the Indian people. As the years passed, Spanish and Indian ways of life in Mexico changed. Many Spaniards were attracted to

"Manuelito," photograph by Charles Bell, copy by Ben Wittick, COURTESY OF THE MUSEUM OF NEW MEXICO IN THE SPECIAL COLLECTIONS LIBRARY, NORTHERN ARIZONA UNIVERSITY, #NAU-417-17

"Cayatanita, Brother of Manuelito, 1874,"
photograph by Charles M. Bell, COURTESY
OF THE SMITHSONIAN INSTITUTION NATIONAL
ANTHROPOLOGICAL ARCHIVES, #2389

the Indian cultures of Mexico. Spaniards and Indians often intermarried and had children. The Spaniards called these children mestizos. Over the years, the number of mestizos in Mexico grew. At first, the mestizo way of life was part Spanish and part Indian, but it soon became an entirely different culture. Mestizos used Spanish tools and raised Spanish livestock, yet they also used traditional Indian tools and foods as well. When they spoke Spanish, they mixed Aztec and other Indian words into the language. Although the mestizos believed in the Spanish religion, they changed it to fit some of their traditional Indian beliefs. The mestizos became the largest group of people in Mexico and began thinking of themselves as different from the Spaniards. They called themselves Mexicans, an Aztec word for Indian peoples of central Mexico.

After three hundred years, the Mexican people became tired of Spanish rule. Spain and the Spanish king were far across the ocean and most of the riches discovered in Mexico were sent to Spain. Many Spaniards became wealthy, while many Mexicans remained poor. The Mexicans were also tired of Spaniards telling them that Spanish people in Mexico had more rights than the mestizos. The mestizos wished to run their own country. They wanted all Mexicans to have the same rights. They hoped to use the riches of Mexico to help the Mexican people. Finally in 1821, the Mexican people revolted and forced the Spaniards to leave their land. The Mexicans chose their own leaders and renamed their new country Mexico. What are now known as Arizona, New Mexico, California, Texas, Utah, Colorado, and most of Nevada were also part of this new country. After the Mexican Revolution, the Spanish leaders and soldiers in New Mexico served the country of Mexico instead of the king of Spain.

Narbona and other headmen soon learned that the Mexicans were much like the Spaniards. The Mexican soldiers raided Navajo settlements, just as the Spaniards had. As before, Navajo warriors fought back, striking at towns and ranches across New Mexico. The New Mexican leaders were unable to stop the Navajo raids. Even with Pueblo help, the soldiers weren't able protect their people. Many ranchers began banding together to defend themselves against Navajo attacks and to raid Navajos for stock and slaves.

In spite of the fighting, Narbona believed he and the Mexican governor could make peace. It was one way to protect his people and property. Manuelito felt differently; he was anxious to attack the New Mexicans. Still, Narbona chose to go to Santa Fe for a peace meeting and Narbona and other Navajo leaders, along with Manuelito and a group of warriors, started off. They traveled in secret and stayed away from well-known trails and towns. Narbona

MAP 8: In 1823, Mexico included much of what is now part of the Unites States of America.

knew that if they were discovered by a band of New Mexican ranchers, they could all be killed. When they arrived in Santa Fe, the Mexican governor was so surprised he agreed to meet with them.

But meetings with Spanish leaders had always been difficult for Navajo headmen. The Spaniards spoke no Navajo and the headmen spoke little or no Spanish. It was hard to understand each other and nearly impossible to explain and discuss problems. When peace meetings ended, each side usually misunderstood the other. That misunderstanding almost always led to more fighting. Narbona feared they would have the same problems this time.

There was a young Mount Taylor Navajo man at the peace meetings in Santa Fe named Antonio Sandoval. Sandoval could speak Navajo and Spanish and he soon played an important role during the meetings with the Mexicans. He skillfully translated and interpreted Spanish words into Navajo and Navajo words into Spanish. When the meetings were over, the Navajo headmen and the Mexican governor signed a peace treaty and the governor promised to find and return Navajo slaves and livestock taken by New Mexican raiders. Narbona agreed to gather and return New Mexican property taken by the Navajos. Young Sandoval offered to help Narbona. Narbona must have been thankful for Sandoval's help. Perhaps working together they could help keep peace.

11
THE STRUGGLE FOR PEACE

Antonio Sandoval belonged to the Tótsohnii Clan, People of the Big Water. His people, the Mount Taylor Navajos, were much like other Navajo bands. At times the Mount Taylor Navajos, the Spanish, and the Pueblos had lived in peace. At other times they had raided each other. War was especially dangerous for Sandoval's people. Most Navajos lived far from their enemies so Spanish and Pueblo raiders had to travel many days to reach Navajo camps. But the Mount Taylor Navajos lived close to the Spaniards and Pueblos and the Spaniards knew the Mount Taylor area well. When fighting between Navajos and Spanish settlers started, Sandoval's people were usually the first ones the soldiers attacked.

Before Antonio was born, Spanish priests had tried to start a mission near Mount Taylor. They wanted the Mount Taylor Navajos to live at the mission. The priests planned to gather the Navajos into a village, have them work at the mission, and teach them about the Spanish religion. Sandoval's people had no use for the mission or the Spanish god. They wanted to be free to live their own way of life. Finally the priests gave up and left but other Spaniards came to live at the foot of Mount Taylor and Hispanic ranchers and farmers settled in the valleys below the sacred mountain. They started the town of Cebolleta and soldiers built a fort there. When the Spanish governor began giving settlers land around Mount Taylor, Sandoval's people joined other Navajos in attacking Cebolleta and the surrounding farms and ranches. The fight was long and fierce. Because they were so close to the Spanish settlements, the Mount Taylor Navajos suffered more from the fighting than other Navajos. They finally had to retreat to the top of the steep-sided mesas around Mount Taylor and build stone walls along the cliffs for safety.

When Antonio Sandoval was small, his father returned from a raid with a captured Hispanic girl. She became part of Antonio's family and she thought of Antonio as a little brother. She learned much about Navajo life from him but she also taught him much about Hispanic life. Antonio's sister even taught him to speak Spanish.

"Indians, Navajo, Biography, (men, unidentified), Navajo warrior with weapons," photographer unknown, COURTESY OF THE DENVER PUBLIC LIBRARY, WESTERN HISTORY DEPARTMENT, F# 22762

"E. San Francisco Street, view looking east, Santa Fe, New Mexico, 1865," photographer unknown, COURTESY OF THE U.S. ARMY SIGNAL CORPS COLLECTION IN THE MUSEUM OF NEW MEXICO, #11330

When he was old enough, Antonio went raiding with the other young men of his band. He brought back captured slaves and livestock. By 1824, Antonio and his family had hundreds of sheep, goats and horses. They farmed huge corn fields on the slopes of Mount Taylor. As Sandoval became older and richer, he better understood the dangers of war. War could destroy his family and everything he had. He decided to make peace with the Spaniards. Thanks to his sister, Antonio could speak Spanish well and he was able to translate for the headmen at the peace meeting in Santa Fe, as mentioned before. His skill in speaking Spanish also allowed him to make friends with many New Mexicans around Mount Taylor. He began visiting Cebolleta and trading with the settlers. When he visited the governor in Santa Fe, he made a point of wearing New Mexican clothing. Sandoval spoke Spanish so well, the Mexican governor thought of him as a friend. To show his friendship, Antonio Sandoval worked with the governor to keep peace between the Mount Taylor Navajos and the New Mexicans. After some time, the governor even made Sandoval a captain in the Mexican army.

Sandoval and Narbona worked together to keep the promises they made with Governor Chacón. They believed that if they did, the Mexicans would keep their promises, too. In 1833, Sandoval and Narbona traveled through Navajo country. They asked each Navajo band they visited to stop raiding and live in peace. The headmen persuaded several bands to give them captured New Mexican livestock and slaves. Then Narbona and Sandoval returned to Santa Fe and handed the livestock and prisoners over to the governor's soldiers.

Sandoval and Narbona had kept their promises, but the fighting went on. Governor Chacón hadn't been able to keep his promises. No New Mexicans returned livestock to the Navajos.

"Unidentified Navajo man, Bosque Redondo era, ca. 1864-1868," photographer unknown, COURTESY OF THE MUSEUM OF NEW MEXICO, #38200

The Mexican soldiers failed to find captured Navajo women and children and return them to their families because most New Mexicans weren't willing to give up their Navajo slaves. They felt their Navajo slaves had a better life with them than with Navajo people. To make things worse, some New Mexicans and Navajos didn't want peace. They were getting rich from fighting so they ignored the peace treaty and continued raiding. Once in a while, New Mexican raiders even attacked the Mount Taylor Navajos. That angered Sandoval, but he still believed he had done the best he could to keep his people safe. He knew some New Mexican raiders didn't care which Navajos they attacked. They could still sell the livestock and prisoners in Santa Fe. Even so, he believed that his people were safe from Mexican military expeditions. The Mexican governor trusted Sandoval and had ordered his soldiers to leave the Mount Taylor Navajos alone.

After all his work for peace, Narbona soon realized that the treaty with the Mexican governor had failed. Mexican leaders accused the Navajo leaders of breaking their promises. Once more, Mexican soldiers attacked the Navajos. New Mexicans raised their own armies and raided Navajo homes for slaves. Manuelito and many of the Chuska Navajos wanted to strike back at the New Mexicans. They wanted to take revenge for the New Mexican raids and try to replace some of their lost livestock. Although Narbona tried to talk him out of going to war, Manuelito began leading Navajo warriors on raids again. Worse still, Ute and Comanche war parties were raiding the Chuska Navajos as well. Each day Narbona heard terrible news. Navajo children were kidnapped. Navajo livestock was driven off. Whole families just vanished. Narbona had to do something to protect his people.

Narbona gathered the younger boys in his band. He told them to go to the mesas and mountain tops to watch for enemies. The boys would be his people's sentries. At the same time, Narbona sent groups of warriors riding out across the land, scouting for enemy war parties. Once they spotted the enemy, the scouts could warn their people. That gave Navajo families plenty of time to escape with their herds into the mountains. It also gave Narbona and his warriors enough time to prepare to ambush the enemy before they could attack Chuska Navajo homes.

The old headman's plan worked well. In October, 1835 his men ambushed and killed almost fifty New Mexican slave raiders. Later that year, Narbona, Manuelito and two hundred warriors surprised an army of New Mexican raiders at Washington Pass, deep in the Chuska Mountains. The Navajos hid along the clifftops above and watched as the raiders entered the narrow pass. Once the New Mexicans were in the canyon, Narbona's men rolled huge boulders and logs down on them, then sent stones, arrows and a few gun shots into the confused crowd below. The raiders were so surprised, they stampeded out of the canyon and never came back. Narbona's plan also protected the Chuska Navajos from enemy Indian war parties. During one ambush, Narbona's men attacked a Comanche war party and captured their horses. Of all the fine captured Comanche horses, Narbona chose the dead Comanche leader's Appaloosa pony for himself.

By 1840, Navajos were raiding towns and ranches across the Southwest and into northern Mexico. The Mexican army hadn't been able to stop the Navajo attacks. Many New Mexicans had died trying to invade Navajo land. The Mexican leaders began to believe that Antonio Sandoval and the Mount Taylor Navajos were really helping other Navajos raid so they no longer trusted Antonio. Instead, they told Sandoval that if all the Navajos didn't stop fighting, Mexican soldiers would destroy the Mount Taylor Navajos. Sandoval became angry. He felt the Mexicans were unfairly blaming his people for raids by other Navajos. Sandoval knew he had to do something to protect his family and his band.

Antonio learned that other Navajo headmen were planning to hold an important meeting in the Chuska Mountains. When the Mount Taylor headman arrived there, he explained that the Mexicans had threatened to destroy his people because other Navajos were raiding. Sandoval blamed some of the Navajo leaders there for the raids that caused his people trouble. There was a loud argument and Manuelito and other headmen accused Antonio of secretly helping the New Mexicans attack Navajos all along. When he left the meeting, Sandoval was furious. He could think of only one way to protect his people. He rode to Santa Fe and told the governor that he and his men wanted to help the Mexican soldiers. The Mount Taylor Navajo would show their friendship by joining the New Mexican side.

The governor agreed. He sent Sandoval sixty soldiers from Cebolleta. Antonio gathered his warriors. Together, the Mount Taylor warriors and the Mexican soldiers raided other Navajos. Sandoval guided Mexican troops through the Navajo country that he knew so well. Sandoval and his men helped destroy hogans and farms, capture Navajo livestock, and take Navajo women and children as slaves. Because he knew so much about Navajo land and the Navajo people, Sandoval had become a dangerous enemy. Many Navajos wanted to kill him. They began calling the Mount Taylor Navajos by a new name. They called them Diné Ana'í, or the Enemy Navajos.

"Washington Pass," from engraving, COURTESY OF THE MUSEUM OF NEW MEXICO HISTORY LIBRARY.

THE AMERICANS

One autumn day in 1846, Antonio Sandoval rode into Narbona's camp. The Chuska Navajos were surprised to see him there. It was dangerous for Sandoval to travel in Navajo country, but Antonio had an important message for Narbona. The Mexican soldiers were gone! A new army was in Santa Fe. The new army's leader wanted to meet with all Navajo headmen. He wanted them to go with Sandoval to Santa Fe and make peace.

"What are these new men called?" Narbona may have asked.

"They are called the Bilagáana," the Mount Taylor headman probably replied, "Americans. They are powerful. Their army easily defeated the Mexican soldiers."

In 1846, what is now known as California, Arizona, Nevada, Utah, New Mexico, and Colorado were still part of Mexico. Texas once had belonged to Mexico, too, but in 1836 the Texans rebelled and started their own country. Later when Texas joined the United States, the Mexican and American leaders began arguing about which parts of Texas belonged to the United States and which were parts of Mexico. Both countries sent soldiers to the Rio Grande River in Texas. When the Mexican and American soldiers began shooting at each other, the United States invaded Mexico. By 1848, the Americans had defeated the Mexican armies and forced their leaders to surrender. Then the Americans took the Southwest from Mexico. New Mexico, Arizona, California, Nevada, Utah, and Colorado became part of the United States of America.

The American army rode into Santa Fe in August, 1846. The leader of the Americans, General Kearny, was anxious to move on and attack Mexico. The general had to make sure the New Mexicans wouldn't rebel against his soldiers in Santa Fe. He hoped his army and the people of New Mexico could be friends. Kearny learned the Navajos and Apaches were at war with the New Mexicans. To earn the New Mexicans' friendship, he promised that his soldiers would protect their ranches and towns. Kearny left Colonel Alexander Doniphan and several hundred soldiers at Santa Fe's

MAP 9: By 1848, the United States/ Mexico borders had shifted greatly.

new American fort, Fort Marcy. Before leaving for California, Kearny ordered Doniphan to force the Navajos to make peace.

Antonio Sandoval offered to help Doniphan make peace with the Navajo people. The Mount Taylor headman agreed to risk his own life and travel to Navajo country. He would invite the Navajo leaders to come to Santa Fe for a peace meeting with Colonel Doniphan. Sandoval rode off towards Navajo country. Weeks passed. When the Mount Taylor headman returned, only four Navajo headmen had agreed to come back with him. Doniphan was disappointed. Most Navajo leaders had refused to travel to Santa Fe. It was too dangerous and they didn't trust Sandoval. There would be no peace meeting.

Narbona thought about what the Mount Taylor headman had told him. Were the Americans really that powerful? Had they defeated the Mexicans? Narbona had to find out. He gathered his weapons, saddled his horse, and called to his men. He was going to Santa Fe. The old headman would see what the Americans were really like!

Narbona and his warriors traveled in secret, following hidden hunting trails through the canyons and mesas. When they reached the Santa Fe Mountains, they camped among the thick pine trees. Narbona searched through the forest until he found a safe place from where he could spy on Fort Marcy far below. For days Narbona watched the fort from his hiding place. He counted the soldiers and their rifles, their wagons and cannons. He noticed the herds of strong cavalry horses and pack mules that filled the fort corrals. At times, rifle shots and the roar of cannon echoed up through the mountains. Finally, Narbona had seen enough. It was dangerous to stay any longer. He and his men quietly slipped away through the forest and headed home.

Colonel Doniphan was unhappy when Sandoval returned with only four Navajo headmen. He ordered Sandoval to guide one of his officers, Captain Reid, and thirty soldiers to Navajo land. Doniphan told Sandoval and Reid to invite the Navajo headmen to a peace meeting at Bear Springs, New Mexico. He warned them that if the headmen refused, the Americans would attack the Navajos. As Sandoval and Captain Reid headed for Navajo country, Doniphan's army prepared for war.

When Sandoval, Reid, and his soldiers reached the Chuska Mountains, they stopped at a spring to water their horses. There they made camp for the evening. After some time, a soldier suddenly spotted a group of Navajo warriors riding toward them. The Americans were surprised, but they remained calm as the Navajo men rode into camp. Sandoval explained that the Ameri-

"Colonel Alexander Doniphan," photographer unknown, COURTESY OF THE SPECIAL COLLECTIONS DEPARTMENT, GENERAL LIBRARY, UNIVERSITY OF NEW MEXICO.

"The Santa Fe Mountains,"
photograph by the author.

cans had come to invite them to make peace. The Navajo men were curious about the newcomers, so they invited the Americans to an Enemy Way Ceremony being held nearby. Pleased, Sandoval and Reid's small band of soldiers went to the ceremony that evening. The Navajos offered to take care of their horses while the Americans were there. The Navajo headmen did everything they could to make their guests comfortable. Americans and Navajos ate together, talked, traded, gave gifts, and danced far into the night. The headmen carefully watched the American soldiers. They seemed quite friendly.

The next morning Narbona, Manuelito, and other headmen met with Captain Reid. Narbona was old and ill, but he rode proudly into camp. During the meeting, the headmen listened patiently as Sandoval translated Reid's words. There wasn't much argument, until one of Narbona's wives stood up.

"What's wrong with all of you?" she scolded the headmen. "Don't trust these soldiers! The Americans want you to go to the peace meeting so they can ambush and kill you. Right now there are only thirty soldiers here. I think we should kill them, before they can make trouble."

Narbona glanced at the crowd. There were nearly two thousand Navajos in camp that morning. Many of them loudly agreed with Narbona's wife. They were anxious to fight, but they hadn't been to Fort Marcy and hadn't seen the many American soldiers, the rifles, the cannons, and the cavalry horses. Quietly, Narbona told his sons to take his wife away from the meeting. There would be no more talk of war. Narbona and the other Navajo leaders agreed to meet Colonel Doniphan at Bear Springs, New Mexico in November.

So on November 21, 1846, Navajo leaders and over five

hundred Navajo people met Colonel Doniphan and his army at Bear Springs. Snow lay heavy on the mesas that morning. Narbona was so ill that his sons had to carry him to the meeting on a stretcher. Colonel Doniphan started by explaining that the United States had conquered New Mexico. All New Mexicans had become United States citizens, and it was now the American army's job to protect their property. Doniphan added that all the Navajo people had become Americans, too. If the Navajo people would end their war with the New Mexicans, the American soldiers would also protect Navajo property.

After some time, a medicine man spoke up. He was Naat'áanii Náádleeł, Becomes Leader Again, from the Tábąąhá, or Water's Edge Clan. The New Mexicans called him Zarcillos Largos, Long Earrings.

"Americans!" Zarcillos Largos began. "We have fought the Mexicans for many years. Now your powerful army has conquered them, just as we wanted to do. Why do you want us to stop fighting our enemies now? We are only doing what you have done. This is our war. If the Americans are fair, they will let us settle our fight by ourselves."

Colonel Doniphan replied that if the Navajo people agreed to sign the treaty, they would get many valuable things by trading with the New Mexicans and the Americans. Navajos would be able to learn many things from the Americans that would help their people. Zarcillos Largos thought for a bit.

"If you have really defeated the Mexicans, we will stop attacking them," he said. "We have no reason to fight with you. We don't want to argue with a powerful nation. Let there be peace between us."

Most of the Navajo leaders agreed with Naat'áanii Náádleeł. Narbona, Manuelito, Zarcillos Largos, Sandoval and ten other headmen signed the Bear Springs Peace Treaty. The Navajo leaders promised to stop their war, allow New Mexicans and Americans to travel safely through Navajo land, and return stolen Mexican livestock and prisoners. The Americans promised to protect Navajo land, homes, and families. Navajos would be able to safely travel to New Mexican towns to trade. The soldiers would punish slave raiders and return kidnapped Navajo women and children. The Americans also agreed to help return stolen Navajo livestock.

After exchanging gifts with the Americans, the Navajos started back to their homes. Narbona had signed treaties before and had heard many promises. The old headman didn't know how long the new peace would last. He did know that the Bear Springs treaty gave his people time to see if the Americans could be trusted.

"U. S. Infantry service uniform, 1835-1851," COURTESY OF THE COLORADO HISTORICAL SOCIETY, F# 32099

BROKEN PROMISES

The Navajo headmen who signed the peace treaty with Colonel Doniphan at Bear Springs agreed to keep peace with the Americans and New Mexicans. Narbona's and Zarcillos Largos' bands, as well as many other Navajos, stopped attacking New Mexican settlements but living in peace was often difficult. Comanche and Ute raiders continued to attack Navajo homes, killing people and stealing horses. Some New Mexicans continued raiding Navajos, kidnapping their children and capturing their livestock. Doniphan had promised that American soldiers would protect Navajo homes from the raiders, but the soldiers were far away and unable to help. The Americans also failed to find and return stolen Navajo livestock and prisoners. Manuelito and others wanted to fight back, but Narbona and Zarcillos Largos convinced them to keep the peace.

Some Navajo bands were still at war with the New Mexicans. Their headmen hadn't been told about the Bear Springs peace meeting. Other Navajo leaders refused to go to Bear Springs. They felt the Americans were helping the New Mexicans fight the Navajos, so they went on attacking New Mexican settlements. There wasn't much that Narbona and Zarcillos Largos could do about the Navajo bands still at war. If other headmen chose to fight, that was their business. Narbona and Zarcillos Largos had only signed the Bear Springs Treaty for their own bands.

When the fighting didn't end, the ranchers demanded that the soldiers punish all the Navajo people. In 1847, American troops marched into the Chuska Mountains, but failed to stop the raiding Navajo bands. After that, the Americans gave New Mexicans permission to raid the Navajos on their own. That made the fighting even worse. New Mexican raiders struck the Chuska Navajos, running off thousands of sheep and horses. Meanwhile the Americans made new plans to invade Navajo country.

The American leaders believed Narbona and the other peaceful headmen had broken the peace treaty. They accused them

"Navajo children in Cañon de Chelly," photographer unknown, COURTESY OF THE ARIZONA HISTORICAL SOCIETY LIBRARY, #15794

of promising to live in peace while they secretly raided the New Mexicans. At the Bear Springs meeting, the Americans had believed Narbona and Zarcillos Largos were the chiefs of all the Navajo people and they thought the headmen had the power to force Navajo bands to stop raiding. Narbona and Zarcillos Largos knew they could only speak for their own bands. They couldn't force anyone to stop fighting. They had to persuade them to keep the peace and return stolen New Mexican livestock and prisoners. Before a Navajo leader signed a treaty, he met with other headmen to discuss making peace. Then the headman met with his people to get their support. Anyone who had any thoughts was allowed to speak. If his band agreed, then the headman felt he could sign the treaty. Navajos respected their headmen and usually listened to their advice.

Narbona, Zarcillos Largos and the Chuska Navajos had kept the peace, but the Americans blamed them for raiding, anyway. In the spring of 1848, two hundred soldiers marched into Navajo country to attack the Navajos. Sandoval guided the Americans, but secretly he sent messengers ahead to warn Navajos that soldiers were coming. That gave families time to escape with their belongings. As it happened, the army found very few Navajos to fight. To protect their people, Narbona, Zarcillos Largos and other peaceful headmen met the Americans near Sanostee and signed another treaty. Narbona sent the soldiers some livestock and returned twelve prisoners he'd gathered from different Navajo bands.

"Kearny's army crossing the Great Plains, 1848," from John Twitchell, *The Leading Facts of New Mexican History*, Torch Press, 1911-1917, COURTESY OF THE MUSEUM OF NEW MEXICO HISTORY LIBRARY

After the 1848 treaty, the fighting between Navajos and New Mexicans almost ceased. On July 5, 1848, Navajo leaders returned a herd of captured horses to the Americans in Santa Fe. On August 24, Navajos turned another group of New Mexican captives over to the soldiers. But during the winter of 1849, New Mexican raiders kidnapped two Navajo girls. Shortly after that, Navajo raiders again attacked New Mexican ranches and settlements. The fighting started once more.

Colonel Washington, the new military governor in Santa Fe, accused Narbona and the peaceful Navajo bands of breaking the 1848 treaty. He even accused Sandoval of raiding the New Mexicans while pretending to be friends with the Americans. Washington didn't put any blame on the New Mexican raiders. Instead, he ordered Sandoval to guide 178 soldiers, 123 New Mexicans, and 60 Pueblo warriors into Navajo land.

On August 29, 1849, Washington's troops attacked Navajo settlements at Naschitti. When the news reached Narbona, he called a meeting of headmen. They hadn't done anything wrong, yet the Americans wanted a fight. Still, Narbona hoped to protect his people by making peace. To show his friendship, he sent fifteen horses, ten mules, and fifty sheep to Washington's camp, but the Americans continued to destroy Navajo homes. That evening they allowed their horses to feed in Navajo cornfields. Dismayed, Narbona sent a message to Colonel Washington. He asked him to stop destroying the people's cornfields and to meet with him at Two Grey Hills. Washington agreed to meet, but refused to stop the cavalry horses from feeding on Navajo corn.

On August 30, Narbona, his group of headmen, and several hundred Navajo warriors met Washington and his army. The old headman could not understand why the Americans were acting in such an unfriendly way. He repeated that his people were living in peace and he explained that the peaceful headmen could not be responsible for other raiding bands. Still, Colonel Washington demanded that Narbona pay for the lost New Mexican livestock and captives. That upset the Chuska headman, but he agreed. He told Washington that the Americans were giving him no choice. The next day, Narbona had his men gather over one thousand sheep, fifteen horses, and a herd of cattle. They drove the animals down to Two Grey Hills and gave them to the Americans. Once more, Narbona met with Colonel Washington. Washington expected him and other Navajo leaders to go to another peace meeting in Canyon de Chelly. Narbona said he was too old and ill to make the trip, but he promised to send a younger leader to take his place.

Just as the meeting was ending, Narbona heard some shouting in the crowd. Sandoval was sitting on horseback, making a speech to a group of mounted Navajo warriors. He rode back and forth, loudly blaming them for starting all the fighting. Many of the warriors were angry and some wanted to shoot Sandoval out of his saddle. They began arguing with the Mount Taylor headman when, suddenly, a New Mexican shouted that one of the Navajo men there was riding a horse that had belonged to him. He claimed it had been stolen from his corral. Things got dangerously out of hand. Narbona left the meeting and rushed into the crowd to calm everyone. Washington demanded that the warrior

Sandoval rode back and forth, accusing the Navajo warriors of breaking the peace with the Americans.

turn the horse over to the New Mexican. As the New Mexican grabbed for the horse, the Navajo reined his pony around and dashed away. All at once the whole camp was in confusion. Colonel Washington shouted an order. The Americans raised their rifles. Like a wave, the crowd of Navajo horsemen turned and galloped off towards the hills. Narbona gripped the reins of his frightened pony, urging his people to stay calm.

"Fire!" Colonel Washington cried.

Smoke flashed from the soldiers' rifles and bullets ripped into the Navajos. Narbona's horse streaked away, its reins flying in the wind. As the Navajo people scattered into the hills, the eighty-three year old Chuska headman stumbled back and fell to the ground. American cannons thundered after the Navajos as they vanished into the hills. When the gun shots faded away, Narbona and seven other Navajos had been killed.

A few days later, Colonel Washington was able to get two headmen to sign another treaty at Canyon de Chelly, but there would be no peace. Narbona, the great Navajo peace leader, was gone forever. Manuelito became headman of the Chuska Navajos. He promised to take revenge on the Americans and New Mexicans for killing his father-in-law.

FORT DEFIANCE

Between 1849 and 1851, Navajos raided settlements across New Mexico and struck ranchers near Sandia Pueblo and at Cebolleta, taking several thousand sheep. Navajo raiders also attacked the Jemez, Zuni, Acoma, Laguna, and Isleta pueblos. When they had the opportunity, warriors shot at American soldiers and drove off Army horses and mules.

Manuelito may have felt that fighting the Americans wasn't as dangerous as Narbona had believed. Navajo war ponies were faster than the big American cavalry horses and Navajo raiders often escaped any soldiers following them. When American troops invaded Navajo land, Navajo scouts spotted them in advance and warned people to take their livestock into hidden canyons and caves. The American soldiers usually burned a few hogans and corn fields, then left. Few Navajos were killed. Manuelito may have thought Narbona was wrong to worry about the soldiers he'd seen at Fort Marcy. Ute, Comanche, and New Mexican raiders were more dangerous enemies than the Americans.

In 1851, the Americans decided to build a fort in the Chuska Mountains that they hoped would stop Navajo raids. They built it at Tséhootsooí and named it Fort Defiance. Fort Defiance stood in the middle of Navajo grazing land. Manuelito and his people wanted to destroy the fort, but they weren't powerful enough to defeat the many soldiers there. However, Fort Defiance didn't stop Manuelito and his men from raiding the New Mexicans. When a Navajo war party left for a raid, they avoided the fort and stayed out of sight. By the time the American soldiers found out about the raid, it was too late. Soldiers would ride out of the fort, destroy a few Navajo camps, then ride back to Fort Defiance. After a time, Navajo families would return and rebuild their destroyed homes. Navajo raiders continued to attack New Mexican and Pueblo settlements.

Although Fort Defiance failed to stop the Navajos' war, a fort on Navajo land worried Zarcillos Largos. His men had raided the fort's supply wagons and had driven off American livestock. Yet when Narbona was alive and working for peace, there had been no

"Heger Drawing of Fort Defiance, ca. 1860," from the Heger Collection, COURTESY OF THE ARIZONA HISTORICAL SOCIETY LIBRARY, #61569

American fort in the middle of Navajo country. Zarcillos Largos knew that the fighting between Navajos and Americans was getting worse. What if the Americans sent even more soldiers to Fort Defiance? Could his people fight them all?

Zarcillos Largos didn't like fighting. He was a medicine man who had worked many years for peace. His family and relatives were suffering because of war so Zarcillos Largos decided to try and make peace once more. He and other Navajo headmen made the risky trip to the American military post at Jemez where they met with the Americans and offered to sign a peace treaty. They told the Americans that they had kept their promises all along and they were bitter about being unfairly blamed for all the fighting. New Mexican raiders had often broken the peace.

"My people are all crying because of the same thing," one Navajo leader explained. "Three of these headmen here are sad because Mexicans stole their children. More than two hundred of our children have been taken. We do not know where they are. We've returned slaves to you eleven times. The Mexicans have returned prisoners to us only once. Do the Americans think that is fair?"

The Americans listened and said they understood, but they did nothing to stop the New Mexicans from raiding Navajo homes. Zarcillos Largos headed home and when he arrived, his wife had frightening news. While he was in Jemez making peace with the

"Navajos at Fort Defiance," photographer unknown, from the Halseth Collection, COURTESY OF THE MUSEUM OF NORTHERN ARIZONA, #MS 79

Americans, New Mexican raiders had attacked his family at Ganado. They had killed his nephews and kidnapped several women and children. His wife had barely escaped being captured herself. Zarcillos Largos wondered if his people would ever be able to live peacefully.

In 1853, the Americans sent a soldier named Henry Dodge to Fort Defiance as an Indian agent. An Indian agent was supposed to speak for the Navajo people and help them. His job was to help make peace between the Navajos and the Americans. Dodge wasn't the first American Indian agent to work with the Navajo people. There had been others, but they knew very little about Navajo people. The Indian agents had lived in Jemez or Santa Fe, far from Navajo land. Many headmen didn't want to make the dangerous trip to see them and when they did, Zarcillos Largos and other Navajo leaders discovered that the Americans usually blamed them for the fighting and slave raiding. Navajos believed it was useless meeting with them.

But Henry Dodge wasn't like the other agents. He had lived in the Southwest for many years and had been with Colonel Washington's expedition in 1849. He knew something about Navajo land and people. When Dodge arrived at Fort Defiance, he decided not to live at the fort. He hoped to live among the Navajo people and earn their friendship. Dodge built his agency, or home, near Washington Pass at Sheep Springs, several miles from Fort Defiance. Agent Dodge hired Juan Anaya, a Hispanic captive of the Navajos, to show him around the Chuska Mountains and interpret for him. Anaya had been raised by Navajos, so he spoke Navajo as well as Spanish. Together, they visited Navajo camps. Many Navajos were surprised at Henry Dodge's friendliness. The headmen told him about the Navajo people's problems and how he could help them and Dodge promised to do what he could.

After visiting Navajo homes, Dodge returned to his agency at Sheep Springs and wrote several letters to the United States government telling the American leaders that the Navajos wanted peace. He described the huge Navajo farms and herds of livestock he had seen and how hard Navajo people worked. Dodge believed that the Americans could end their war with the Navajos if they helped Navajo people instead of fighting them. He asked the government to send the Navajos farm tools, seeds, and livestock. Dodge even spent much of his own money buying farm tools. As the supplies arrived at Fort Defiance, Agent Dodge handed them out to Navajo families. When Navajo men asked him for a place where they could make iron tools, Dodge offered to build a blacksmith shop at his agency. The Navajo people realized that Henry

Dodge really wanted to help them and they began calling him Bi'éé' Łichíí'ii, Red Shirt.

Zarcillos Largos and Manuelito were pleased with Agent Dodge. They agreed to persuade other headmen to work for peace with the Americans. They trusted Red Shirt. They liked and respected him and felt comfortable visiting him at the agency. They invited him to traditional ceremonies. Before long Zarcillos Largos and Henry Dodge had become good friends. Some say Dodge married one of Zarcillos Largos' nieces. Red Shirt and the headmen worked together to return stolen livestock to the New Mexicans and make sure that the Americans punished New Mexicans who raided Navajo homes. By 1855, almost all the fighting was over. Zarcillos Largos and Henry Dodge had succeeded. They had made peace between the Navajos and the Americans.

Zarcillos Largos hoped peace would last, but in 1856, the old headman learned some bad news. Agent Dodge had been ambushed and killed by Apache warriors while he was on a hunting trip near Zuni. With Dodge gone, Zarcillos Largos' hard work soon began to fall apart. In June of 1858, an argument started over some grazing land near Fort Defiance. There had been a bad drought that year and Manuelito and his people needed the grazing land for their livestock. Major Brooks, the fort commander, insisted that the soldiers needed the grass land to feed their cavalry horses. When Manuelito refused to move his livestock, Brooks had the animals shot dead. Manuelito was furious and would do nothing more for the Americans. Zarcillos Largos explained to Major Brooks that Manuelito expected the Americans to pay him for the animals they had killed but the major refused. Two months passed and unfriendly feelings between Navajos and Americans grew. One August day, a Navajo man visiting Fort Defiance suddenly killed Major Brooks' black slave, then escaped before anyone realized what had happened. That was the end of peace. In September, the American cavalry rode out of Fort Defiance to attack Navajo camps. They were joined by groups of New Mexicans, Utes, and Pueblos. Soldiers charged into Canyon de Chelly and destroyed every Navajo home they could find. They even attacked Zarcillos Largos' people camped north of Fort Defiance. The old headman and his men rushed for their weapons as their women and children ran for safety. On horseback, Zarcillos Largos rode among his men, encouraging them to protect their families. The old headman was wounded three times, but each time he climbed back on his horse to lead his warriors. When the women and children had finally escaped, Zarcillos Largos' men retreated into the hills, taking their badly wounded headman with them.

"Canyon del Muerto," photograph of illustration by R. H. Kern, COURTESY OF THE MUSEUM OF NEW MEXICO HISTORY LIBRARY

Barboncito was also called Hastiin Dághaa'

The Americans' war had hurt the Navajo people. Troops had destroyed much of the Navajo fall harvest and many families would go hungry that winter. Zarcillos Largos and other headmen decided to sign another peace treaty with the Americans. One of the headmen who signed the treaty was a medicine man named Barboncito. Navajo people called him Hastiin Dághaa', or Moustached Man. He belonged to the Ma'iideeshgizhnii', Coyote Pass People clan. Barboncito's people lived in Canyon de Chelly and although the Americans had destroyed many of his people's homes and farms, Barboncito helped Zarcillos Largos try to bring peace to the land. During the following months, they gathered over six thousand sheep to give to the Americans at Fort Defiance. American soldiers continued to threaten their people and New Mexican and Ute war parties went on raiding Navajo camps. At last Zarcillos Largos and Barboncito gave up. They felt they had done everything they could to make peace.

Zarcillos Largos was very concerned about his people. One day while he was praying, he had a vision. The vision was so horrible, he couldn't forget it. Later, Zarcillos Largos learned there would be a leaders' meeting at Chinle. Anxiously he left to attend the meeting where the leaders would decide whether to make peace or fight with the Americans. Many of the headmen gave reasons to go on fighting the Americans. Barboncito and Manuelito were even making plans to attack Fort Defiance. Zarcillos Largos listened. At last, he spoke and told them about his vision.

"I have seen this, my brothers. I don't even want to think about it, but it keeps coming back to me. I saw darkness everywhere. Our sacred mountains were hidden in black clouds. All across our land, my people were all gone. There wasn't a breath to be heard. All I could hear was the howl of coyotes and I felt the wind of death in my face. That is what I have seen."

When Zarcillos Largos sat down, a hush fell over the meeting. The vision upset many of the headmen. Manuelito finally broke the silence. The time had come. The Navajos had to drive the Americans out of their land before Zarcillos Largos' vision came true. Sadly, Zarcillos Largos rode back home. The old headman's days of peace making were over.

LAND ON FIRE

In 1860, Manuelito and Barboncito began their war on the Americans at Tséhootsoí. On January 17th, two hundred Navajos attacked the Fort Defiance hay camp. They burned the soldiers' hay stacks and captured a herd of cattle. On February 8th, warriors attacked a troop of soldiers guarding the fort's livestock.

Manuelito, Barboncito, and other Navajo war leaders felt the time was right to attack Fort Defiance itself. On the night of April 29th, 1860, a thousand warriors silently surrounded the fort. Except for a few sentries, all of the soldiers slept. Suddenly guns flashed in the darkness and the Navajos charged. Before the soldiers were awake, Navajo warriors had rushed into the fort gardens. They took cover behind fences, wood piles, and adobe walls. Arrows flew towards the soldiers' barracks. The confused Americans fired back from open windows and from behind doors. The battle lasted for several hours and when dawn finally came, the Navajo warriors retreated into the hills. One soldier had been killed, two others wounded. The Navajos hoped they'd given the Americans a good scare. Perhaps the soldiers would decide to leave Navajo land.

In spite of the Navajo attack on the fort, the soldiers remained at Fort Defiance. By the winter of 1861 there was more bad news

"Fort Defiance-Canyoncito Bonito, 1857," photograph of and illustration from W. H. Davis, *"El Gringo" or New Mexico and Her People*, Rydal Press, Santa Fe, New Mexico, 1938, COURTESY OF THE SPECIAL COLLECTIONS DEPARTMENT, GENERAL LIBRARY, UNIVERSITY OF NEW MEXICO

"Fort Wingate, New Mexico, March, 1890," photograph by Ben Wittick, COURTESY OF THE SCHOOL OF AMERICAN RESEARCH COLLECTIONS IN THE MUSEUM OF NEW MEXICO, #15777

for the Navajo people. Manuelito learned that Zarcillos Largos was dead. He had been returning home alone from visiting the Hopis when Zuni and New Mexican raiders ambushed and killed him. Zarcillos Largos would never see his vision of war come true. Antonio Sandoval, too, would never again help the Americans fight their war against the Navajos. One of Sandoval's unbroken mules had thrown, kicked, and badly injured the old man. He died at his home near Mount Taylor. Manuelito may not have cared much about Sandoval's death since they had been enemies for many years. However, Zarcillos Largos' murder angered Manuelito. He promised to continue his fight with the Americans.

At last Manuelito's hopes seemed to come true. On April 25th, 1861, the American troops left Fort Defiance. They marched into the southern hills and didn't come back. Fort Defiance was deserted. American soldiers no longer threatened the Navajo people. Manuelito, Barboncito, and most headmen hoped their bands would finally be able to live in peace. Fighting had made farming and raising livestock nearly impossible but now the people could rebuild their homes, farms, and herds. Manuelito's people and many other bands stopped fighting. Other bands did not. Some Navajos believed, with the Americans gone, it would be easier to raid the New Mexican ranches.

The Americans had left Fort Defiance, but they were still in the area. The soldiers went to Fort Lyons, later called Fort Wingate, near Bear Springs. The American leaders were still worried about the threat of Navajo raids, but they were more worried about a new and bigger threat. The Americans were moving troops back towards Santa Fe to get ready for a great battle. Texan soldiers were invading New Mexico! The bloody Civil War had begun.

The war between the North and South began when the southern states of America decided to start their own country. The North

Map 10: The Confederate States of America, 1861-1864

"Bvt. Brig. Gen. James H. Carleton, ca. 1868," photographer unknown, COURTESY OF THE MUSEUM OF NEW MEXICO, #22938

claimed that was against the law. The Southern states called themselves the Confederacy. The Confederacy tried to conquer New Mexico, but Northern soldiers defeated them at Glorieta Pass, near Santa Fe. At that time, the Civil War was the biggest war ever fought. Many new weapons were invented and used. Some of these weapons were iron battleships, submarines, and the Gatling gun, a large machine gun that sat on two wagon wheels.

While the U.S. Army was busy fighting the Texans, they were unable to stop raids. Though most Navajo bands tried to live peacefully, some Navajos raided their enemies. Of course, Navajo enemies were free to raid as well. Between 1861 and 1864, New Mexican, Ute, Comanche, Jicarilla Apache, and Pueblo raiders swept across Navajo land like fire. They did not care if they attacked peaceful or raiding Navajo bands. No one was safe. Families were afraid to travel, herd sheep, or work in their gardens. Raiders tore down hogans and trampled farms and captured thousands of sheep, cattle, and horses. They kidnapped many Navajo children since they could sell a healthy Navajo boy or girl to a New Mexican family for as much as four hundred dollars. Many Navajo people lost everything they had. They were homeless, hungry, and always hiding from their enemies. Some Navajo warriors began raiding New Mexican livestock again just to feed their families. Most Navajo men stayed busy protecting their homes, wives, and children. When American troops defeated the Texans at Glorieta Pass, they returned to attacking the Navajos. It seemed as if all Navajo country burned from war. Manuelito and Barboncito realized it was a war their people were slowly losing.

In 1862, General James Carleton was commander of the American troops in New Mexico. Now that the Texans invading New Mexico had been beaten, General Carleton planned to stop the many wars between Indians and New Mexicans in the South-

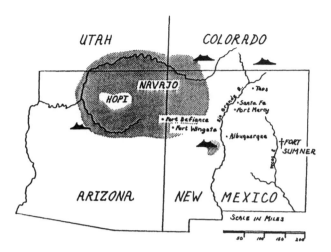

MAP 11: United States military forts in New Mexico Territory, circa 1864.

"Fort Sumner, New Mexico, Bosque Redondo era, ca. 1864-68," photographer unknown, COURTESY OF THE U. S. ARMY SIGNAL CORPS COLLECTION IN THE MUSEUM OF NEW MEXICO, #28533

west. He believed that there were only two ways Indians and Americans could live in peace. Like other American military leaders at that time, Carleton believed that Indian tribes would have to leave their traditional lands and live on a reservation, or the Army would have to destroy them.

General Carleton was especially anxious to conquer the Navajo tribe. He accused all Navajos of being warlike and he believed Navajo leaders couldn't be trusted. Carleton planned to use American troops to force all Navajos to leave their traditional land and move to a reservation. The Navajo reservation would be in eastern New Mexico, along the salty Pecos River. The general had his men build a fort there and he named it Fort Sumner. Once the Navajos were at Fort Sumner, he would force them to change their way of life. Carleton felt that the Navajo people would only survive if they forgot their traditional way of life and learned to live as Americans did. At Fort Sumner, Navajos would learn to farm and live in small towns like Americans. They would wear American clothes and learn American jobs. Navajo children would go to school, learn to speak English, and believe in the Americans' religion. The general believed that once Navajos had forgotten their language and culture, they would become peaceful.

General Carleton told his leaders in Washington that he believed there was gold and silver on Navajo land. When the Navajos had been moved, settlers would be able to mine these riches. Americans would be free to settle Navajo grazing lands, build railroads, farms, and towns among the mountains and mesas. There was no gold or silver on Navajo land, but Carleton may have believed there was. He hoped it would get American leaders to support his plan.

Carleton knew it wouldn't be easy conquering the Navajo people because they were the largest Indian group in the Southwest. Many Spanish, Mexican, and American soldiers had tried before, but had failed. Although the U. S. Army was powerful, the general realized the Army would need help from traditional Navajo enemies. He also needed a scout who knew Navajo people and their land to guide the American military expedition. For these reasons, he chose Christopher "Kit" Carson. The Navajos called Kit Carson Adilohii, or Rope Thrower. Carson was a famous mountain man and Army scout familiar with Navajo country. He had lived in Taos, New Mexico for many years and had been a Ute and Taos Indian agent. He was liked by the Utes, Jicarillas, and New Mexicans. Carleton knew that if any one could get the New Mexicans and Utes to help his soldiers invade Navajo land, Kit Carson could.

Navajo leaders soon learned of General Carleton's plans. Barboncito and his brother Delgadito traveled to Santa Fe to meet with the general. They told Carleton they had always wanted peace. They blamed much of the fighting on the New Mexicans and a few outlaw Navajos. The headmen wanted the American soldiers to help stop enemy raids. Their people were suffering. General Carleton refused and ordered Barboncito and Delgadito to surrender immediately and take their people to Fort Sumner. Later in April of 1863, Barboncito and Carleton met again at Fort Wingate. Barboncito offered to help the soldiers stop any outlaw Navajos who were attacking New Mexican settlements. Again, General Carleton refused. He told Barboncito that the Navajos would only have peace if they moved to Fort Sumner.

"You and your people have until July 20th to surrender," he warned the headman. "If you don't, the soldiers will destroy you."

"I will never leave my own country," Barboncito replied, "even if that means I will be killed."

When the meeting was over, Barboncito and the other Navajo peace leaders left Fort Wingate and headed home with the bad news. Soon hundreds of American soldiers would be returning to Fort Defiance.

"Col. Christopher "Kit" Carson, St. Louis, Missouri, December, 1864," photographer unknown, COURTESY OF THE MUSEUM OF NEW MEXICO, #7151

THE LONG WALK

It was a hot July day in 1863. Manuelito's men stood guard in the hills above Tséhootsoí. Suddenly they spotted a dust cloud rising in the south. The Americans! Kit Carson and seven hundred soldiers were returning to Fort Defiance. The long line of troops, pack mules, and wagons stretched across the valley.

Manuelito and Barboncito grimly watched Carson and his soldiers at Fort Defiance. They knew many Navajo bands were already suffering from enemy raids. Each day war parties attacked Navajo camps. Families were afraid to go back to their homes. Many of their homes had been burned and much of their livestock had been stolen. Ute raiders were especially dangerous. Kit Carson had encouraged the Utes to raid the Navajos. He paid the Utes money for stolen Navajo livestock and allowed them to keep Navajo prisoners. So Ute warriors roamed Navajo land and attacked whoever they found. The headmen knew that soon the soldiers would be attacking Navajo homes, too.

At first, the Americans did little harm to Navajo people. Rope Thrower's troops destroyed the empty Navajo homes in the valley

"Ute Indians- Ute Customs, couple on horseback," photographer unknown, COURTESY OF THE UTAH STATE HISTORICAL SOCIETY, #970.72 P.1

but few Navajo people were killed or captured. Still, the Navajo men fought back. They attacked a group of soldiers rounding up Navajo horses and killed their officer. Warriors raided the Fort Defiance corral and ran off a large herd of horses. That didn't stop Kit Carson for long. In August of 1863, he led his soldiers across Navajo land. He split his men up into small, fast riding groups and they destroyed every Navajo camp they found, but they still weren't able to capture many Navajo people. Most families were able to stay out of the soldiers' way. By September, Carson's men had captured only fifty Navajos. General Carleton was angry. He ordered Rope Thrower to attack Barboncito's band in Canyon de Chelly.

November came. Dark clouds hung over the Chuska Mountains and cold winds rushed through Canyon de Chelly. Winter was coming early, but the Ute and American raiders still attacked Navajo people. Some Navajo bands were running out of food. Their enemies had destroyed their crops and livestock. Barboncito's brother, Delgadito, realized his band wouldn't survive the coming winter. Unhappily, he decided to surrender to the soldiers at Fort Defiance and Kit Carson transferred them to Fort Sumner but Barboncito swore he would never surrender. Just as Carson's soldiers were ready to invade Canyon de Chelly, Barboncito's warriors chased off all the army mules. Carson's soldiers needed those mules to carry their supplies so the American cavalry raced after the raiders, but a heavy snow storm turned them back. Barboncito's people butchered and ate all the mules. Rope Thrower's attack would have to wait.

"Navajo, Barboncito, ca. 1868," photographer unknown, COURTESY OF THE MUSEUM OF NEW MEXICO, #48716

On January 6th, 1864, the Americans were finally ready. Kit Carson led almost four hundred heavily armed soldiers out of the fort and they marched into Canyon de Chelly. Deep snow covered the mesas and the valley below. A sharp wind froze fingers and ears but that didn't bother the Americans. Kit Carson knew winter was on their side. Many Navajos were hungry and freezing and Carson hoped his army would conquer them. His army trudged through the canyon destroying one abandoned camp after another. The soldiers burned the hogans, tore down the corrals, destroyed food

"U. S. Army troops, Fort Sumner, New Mexico, Bosque Redondo era, ca. 1864-1868," photographer unknown, COURTESY MUSEUM OF NEW MEXICO, #23128

supplies, and filled up water holes with rocks and dirt. For sixteen days, Kit Carson's army destroyed everything in their path. At last the Americans reached the Chinle area. Rope Thrower made camp and waited for the Navajos to give up.

Many Navajos realized they would not survive the winter. They had no livestock. Their homes were in ashes, crops destroyed, the children wore rags, and there were so many enemies, people were afraid to light fires to keep warm. Many Navajos had no choice. Families and bands began surrendering to Rope Thrower. Other people straggled into Fort Defiance and Fort Wingate to give up. The soldiers gave the Navajos food and blankets and this surprised the people. They thought the soldiers wanted to kill them. When this news spread among the Navajos, more people surrendered.

Before long, Delgadito, who had just returned from a visit for Fort Sumner, appeared at Fort Defiance. He told the Navajos that there were food, clothes, and safe homes there and there were many soldiers to protect the Navajos from their enemies. Delgadito advised the Navajo people to surrender. One by one, Navajo bands journeyed to Fort Defiance and Fort Wingate. Soon both forts were flooded with thousands of Navajo prisoners and the soldiers ran out of food and blankets. General Carleton was amazed. He did not know there were so many Navajo people!

But several Navajo bands refused to give up. Manuelito and his

MAP 12: The Long Walk of the Navajo across the state of New Mexico.

The Navajo surrender to the military.

"Fortress Rock, Canyon de Chelly," *photograph by author*, COURTESY OF THE NAVAJO NATION.

people migrated into Hopi country. When Carson's attack on Canyon de Chelly was over, Manuelito's band returned to the Chuska Mountains. The men remained ready for war. If the soldiers attacked them, the Chuska Navajos planned to give them a good battle. Barboncito and his band remained free, too. Three hundred of his men, women, and children were hidden safely on top of Fortress Rock in Canyon de Chelly. Fortress Rock was a giant butte with tall, steep sides. Barboncito's band used ladder poles to climb to the top. Then they pulled the ladders up behind them, so no one could follow. The American soldiers knew the Navajos were there. They surrounded Fortress Rock, but couldn't find a way up. There was no water on top of the rock, but there was a water hole at the bottom. The soldiers guarded it day and night and assumed Barboncito's people would surrender or die from thirst. Yet when night came, Hastiin Dághaa's men took up empty water jugs and silently climbed down the cliffs. They tied long yucca ropes to the jugs, lowered the pots into the water hole, filled them, and raised them back up again. The Navajo men were so careful the American guards never realized they had been tricked. After a month, the Americans finally left. Barboncito's band came down from Fortress Rock and they migrated towards the Little Colorado River, hoping the soldiers would never find them.

By March of 1864, over five thousand Navajos were being held by the soldiers as prisoners. Groups of Navajo captives began the

"Tom Toslino as he arrived at the Training School, Carlisle, Pennsylvania, ca. 1880," photograph by John N. Choate, COURTESY OF THE MUSEUM OF NEW MEXICO, #43501

"Manuelito Segundo, son of Manuelito and Juanita," photographer unknown, COURTESY OF THE MUSEUM OF THE AMERICAN INDIAN, HEYE FOUNDATION, #34826

long march to Fort Sumner, several hundred miles away. The Americans only had a few wagons and the Navajo prisoners had very few horses so almost all the people had to travel on foot. Soon their moccasins fell apart and their clothes and blankets turned to rags. When a snow storm rushed down on them, many Navajo people fell sick and died. They also became ill from the strange foods the soldiers gave them. The Navajos didn't know how to use white flour and coffee beans. They mixed the flour with water and drank it. They tried boiling the hard coffee beans in a stew. That gave the Navajos painful stomach cramps. Old people and young children fell by the trail. If they couldn't go on, the soldiers shot them or left them behind to freeze to death.

The ragged prisoners struggled on. Coyotes began following them and crows circled overhead, waiting for someone to die. The line of struggling prisoners became so long the Army couldn't protect them from enemy attacks and New Mexican raiders attacked and carried away children. Still the soldiers forced the Navajos to march.

The headmen wondered if they should have listened to Delgadito's promises. They were suffering more on the Long Walk to Fort Sumner than they had suffered in their own land. Their people were hungry, cold, sick, and sore, and over three hundred Navajos had died on the march, yet they weren't even near Fort Sumner yet. It might have been better to have stayed in Navajoland. Now it was too late. The headmen had only one hope left. They prayed there would be food, clothes, homes, and safety at Fort Sumner.

HWÉELDI-FORT SUMNER

Canyon de Chelly was empty. Only rings of gray ashes along the canyon floor showed where Navajo homes had once stood. As Barboncito gazed into the empty canyon, he remembered Zarcillos Largos' vision.

"Across the land, all our people were gone. Not a breath moved. All I heard was the howl of coyotes."

Zarcillos Largos' words had come true. Many Navajos had been taken to Fort Sumner and those who hadn't surrendered were scattered across the land, trying to find some place safe from their enemies. Many were sick and starving. Barboncito's people and their livestock had survived Kit Carson's winter war, but they lived in fear of their enemies. Each day Barboncito expected the Utes or New Mexicans to attack his band and steal their livestock. How could he best protect them? Would they be safer at Fort Sumner, as Delgadito had claimed?

Barboncito wasn't worried about his people. He felt they could remain free and survive by hunting and gathering. But Barboncito realized that his people's livestock probably wouldn't survive. Sheep, goats, and cattle wouldn't last long searching through the Chuska mountain forests for food. Barboncito's herds needed a lot of grass. Good grazing lands, such as the mountain meadows, the canyon floors, and the high mesa plains, were out in the open and dangerous. People who herded their hungry animals there endangered their whole band. The animals were usually spotted by Ute and New Mexican raiders and if raiders spotted a Navajo herd, they knew a Navajo band was nearby. They often attacked the band and ran off the band's livestock. The herds also slowed people down as they tried to escape. Barboncito knew his people and their animals wouldn't survive together so he pondered how he could save their livestock.

At last Barboncito had an idea. He would surrender and take their animals to Fort Sumner and perhaps there they could safely graze, while his people remained free in Navajo country. The headman knew that someday the fighting would stop. When the war

"Woman nursing with child," photographer unknown, COURTESY OF SPECIAL COLLECTIONS, UNIVERSITY OF ARIZONA LIBRARY.

"Counting Indians-Navajo captives under guard, Fort Sumner, New Mexico, Bosque Redondo era, ca. 1864-68," photographer unknown, COURTESY OF THE U. S. ARMY SIGNAL CORPS COLLECTION IN THE MUSEUM OF NEW MEXICO, #28534

"Group of Navajo Indians, Fort Sumner, New Mexico, Bosque Redondo era, ca. 1864-68" photographer unknown, COURTESY OF THE MUSEUM OF NEW MEXICO. #38191

"Navajo, woman and baby, Bosque Redondo era, ca. 1864-1868," photographer unknown, COURTESY OF THE MUSEUM OF NEW MEXICO, #3242

was over, he would bring the herds back to Canyon de Chelly.

In August of 1864, Barboncito and a few of his people surrendered at Fort Wingate. They had brought fifteen hundred head of sheep with them. Barboncito's group and their livestock joined other Navajos on the Long Walk to Fort Sumner. Weeks passed. Finally the Navajos arrived at the fort. When Barboncito first saw the reservation at Fort Sumner, his heart fell. If only he'd headed west with his livestock to join Manuelito, instead!

Fort Sumner stood at a place New Mexicans called Bosque Redondo, or Circle Grove. The Navajos there called the place Hwéeldi, "the fort." Navajos had helped build the fort, but they couldn't live there. Instead, they lived on the wide plain that surrounded the fort. The plain was flat, dry, and bare. Hundreds of Navajo camps were spread across the land. Navajo families lived in brush covered holes in the ground, or in huts made of sticks, old canvas, and dried cow hides. There were no trees or wood for building hogans. People had to walk for miles just to get firewood. Everywhere he looked, Barboncito saw Navajos in rags. Skinny children wandered around dressed in dirty flour sacks.

Like Barboncito, many Navajos still had livestock when they had surrendered to the Americans. When they arrived at Hwéeldi, whatever animals they had left soon starved. There was very little grass and water from the nearby Pecos River was bitter with alkali. Sheep and horses became sick and died when they drank it.

The Navajo people were suffering almost as badly as their animals. Pecos River water also made Navajos ill when they drank it. Some died. Navajos were dying from hunger, too. General Carleton expected Navajos to raise their own food on farms. The Navajos had agreed to work on the reservation farms, but they feared their families would go hungry before the crops were ready to harvest. Until harvest time came, Carleton ordered his soldiers to

"Navajo Indian captives husking corn, Fort Sumner, New Mexico, Bosque Redondo era, ca. 1864-68," photographer unknown, COURTESY OF THE MUSEUM OF NEW MEXICO, #38205

"Navajos at the Provost Marshall's office," photographer unknown, COURTESY OF THE NATIONAL ARCHIVES, #111-SC-87966

hand out rations to each Navajo family. They usually didn't hand out enough food, however, so families went hungry. Many of the foods were new to the Navajos. They were used to traditional foods and didn't know how to use white flour, sugar, salt, and coffee beans. The strange American foods made people sick. Many Navajos had to hunt for rabbits, mice, and prairie dogs to feed themselves. Men secretly left the reservation to hunt for antelope or deer. Sometimes they would risk taking a cow from a New Mexican ranch. Although they were hungry, Navajos at Hwéeldi seldom butchered a sheep. They hoped to save most of their stock, but New Mexican raiders and coyotes often got them instead. Often, the raiders attacked Navajo camps and kidnapped children.

Barboncito joined the men working in the fields. He helped dig the irrigation ditches that brought Pecos River water to the Navajo farms. He dug, planted, and hoed, while soldiers stood guard over the workers. Before long plants sprouted and grew strong. Just as Barboncito began to hope there would be a fine harvest, a sudden hail storm shredded the plants and beat them into the ground. Then cutworms destroyed much of the corn that had survived the hail. That year the Navajo farm harvest was small and the soldiers had to hand out rations again. Food supplies at the fort store began to run low. To save food, the Americans gave each family ration tickets. Each time they went, they received less and less food for their tickets. Some Navajo men began to counterfeit tickets to get extra food for their families. The soldiers soon discovered the counterfeit tickets and arrested the men. Once more their families went hungry.

General Carleton hoped he could get the Navajos to live more like the Pueblos, so he planned to make them live in square adobe houses built along wide American-style streets but Navajos refused to live in that way. They enjoyed living among their relatives in

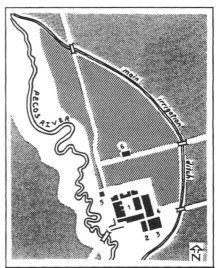

1) Fort Sumner Quarters 2) Sutler's Store 3) Cavalry Stables 4) Indian Issue House 5) Provost Marshal's Office 6) Indian Hospital   ///// Indian Farms   ░░░ Navajo Settlements   ⊐⊏ Bridge

"Hwéeldi-Fort Sumner" map by author, adapted from Gerald Thompson, *The Army and the Navajo*, University of Arizona Press, Tucson, 1982

"Two unidentified Navajo girls, Bosque Redondo era, ca. 1864-68," photographer unknown, COURTESY OF THE MUSEUM OF NEW MEXICO, #38197

"Hoskininnii and woman, Oljato, Utah, ca. 1908," photograph by Young (?), COURTESY OF THE ARIZONA STATE MUSEUM UNIVERSITY OF ARIZONA, #30359

"U. S. Army troops, Fort Sumner, New Mexico, Bosque Redondo era, ca. 1864-68," photographer unknown, COURTESY OF THE MUSEUM OF NEW MEXICO, #28537

groups of hogans. Strangers could be dangerous and Navajos didn't trust strangers, even if they were other Navajos. The people hated square houses with doorways that didn't face east. Traditionally, if someone died in a hogan, everyone had to move out. So once there was a death in an adobe house, the Navajo family would refuse to live in it! Carleton was angry with the Navajos, but at last he gave up his plan. He agreed to allow people to live in hogans if they built them in a straight line along the street. Everyone wondered how they would do that. There wasn't any wood to build hogans.

During the summer of 1865, Barboncito secretly left Hwéeldi. He hoped to find out how well his band had survived in Navajo country. He found his people living near Navajo Mountain. They were poor, but they were alive and free. Barboncito continued traveling through Navajoland, visiting other free bands to tell them news about Fort Sumner. He found Manuelito and his band suffering badly. They were sick, starving, wounded, and poor. Raiders had repeatedly attacked them, stealing most of their livestock. The American soldiers threatened them, too. General Carleton had promised a large reward for anyone who could capture the Chuska headman. In spite of these hardships, Manuelito refused to give up.

"I will stay in my own country. I've got nothing to lose but my life. The soldiers can come and take that whenever they please! But I will not go to Hwéeldi."

Before leaving, Barboncito gave Manuelito some hopeful news. He told him that many Navajos were still free. Navajo bands were living near Shonto, on top of Black Mesa and in the Chuska Mountains. A headman named Hoskininni, or Hashkéneiniihii, He Angrily Hands Them Out, was living at Navajo Mountain. Hoskininni had seen a vision. Someday, he said, the Navajo people would return to their homelands. Hoskininni had been able to save over two thousand sheep and one hundred horses. He planned to

hand them out when the people finally returned.

It made Barboncito sad to leave Manuelito and his suffering people, but he was anxious to return to Hwéeldi. Many Navajos there would be excited to hear all the news. Navajos who were still free wanted to hear news of their relatives at Fort Sumner, too. As he headed back to Bosque Redondo, Barboncito planned to make another visit to Navajo country.

Barboncito made several trips between Hwéeldi and Navajoland to encourage his people. In 1866, he found Manuelito's tiny and beaten band camped near Zuni. Hopi warriors had attacked them at Black Mesa. All their livestock had been taken. Manuelito had been shot in the arm and in the side. He knew he couldn't go on and he couldn't bear to see his people suffer so much. Manuelito told Barboncito he was going to surrender. On September 1, 1866 Manuelito and twenty three surviving relatives walked into Fort Wingate. Immediately the soldiers sent them all to Fort Sumner and General Carleton believed his war with the Navajos was finally over.

By October of 1866, Barboncito had joined Manuelito at Hwéeldi. He would make no more trips to Navajoland. He realized he had to help his people survive. As Manuelito recovered from his wounds, Barboncito and other medicine men held ceremonies. Through prayer they urged the Holy People to help the Navajos. Yet the months dragged by and more troubles came. Rain wouldn't fall, the Pecos River dried up, and the farms died. Then a deadly disease called small pox swept through Navajo homes. Over two thousand Navajo men, women and children died. New Mexican and Comanche war parties killed even more people. They raided Navajo camps, attacked wood gatherers, and ran off livestock. In September of 1867, two hundred Comanche warriors even attacked the fort! It was a bloody battle. The soldiers had to give Navajo men weapons to help drive the Comanches away.

Many Navajos tried to escape the death and disease at Hwéeldi. They often left in small groups, while sometimes entire bands of hundreds of people escaped. The people wanted to go home so badly, they were willing to risk the dangers of slave raiders, soldiers, thirst, hunger, and cold. Many of them were never seen again. Some joined bands of Navajo raiders who were still attacking New Mexican settlements in the Fort Sumner area. Although a few Navajos were able to return to their homeland, enemies forced most of them to return to Hwéeldi. By the end of 1867, many Navajos feared the Holy People had left them and that they would all die at Fort Sumner.

"Navajo Chief Manuelito (Pistol Bullet), ca. 1865-70," photographer unknown, COURTESY OF THE MUSEUM OF NEW MEXICO, #23130

"Navajo, Juanita, wife of Manuelito, 1874," photograph by Charles M. Bell, COURTESY OF THE SMITHSONIAN INSTITUTION NATIONAL ATHROPOLOGICAL ARCHIVES, #59435

18 THE TREATY OF 1868

However bad things were at Hwéeldi, Barboncito refused to give up hope. By 1867, some American leaders felt that making the Navajos move to Fort Sumner had been a mistake. They held several meetings with Barboncito, Manuelito, and other headmen. The Americans wanted to know what the headmen thought about living at Bosque Redondo and what should be done about the problems Navajos were having there. Barboncito realized that the Americans were changing their minds about keeping the Navajos at Bosque Redondo. Perhaps his prayers had worked! At each meeting, Barboncito and the headmen repeated that the Navajo people wished to return to their traditional lands. The Americans listened, but made no promises.

One day Theodore Dodd, the Navajo Indian agent at Fort Sumner, brought Manuelito and Barboncito some good news. General Carleton had been fired. The American leaders in Washington, D.C. were unhappy with Carleton's Bosque Redondo reservation. After three years, the Indian farms there still couldn't support the Navajo people. The harvest of 1867 had been very poor and the Americans realized that, once more, they would have to spend money on rations for the Navajos that coming winter. Keeping Navajos at Bosque Redondo cost the American government millions of dollars, yet the Navajo people were in a worse condition than they had ever been in before. It was clear that Carleton's plans for the Navajos had failed. The American leaders in Washington were anxious to find a better plan. They wanted to speak with the Navajo leaders. Dodd instructed Barboncito and Manuelito to get ready for a long journey. They were going to visit the President in Washington, D.C.!

Agent Dodd, Barboncito, and his group of headmen left for Washington in April of 1868. It was the first time Navajos had traveled across the United States. Barboncito gazed through the window as their train chugged across America. Huge farms spread out across the land. Tall cities flashed by, their streets filled with people, horses, and wagons. There were so many Americans!

At last they arrived in Washington and met with several

American leaders. Finally, Barboncito and his group met with President Andrew Johnson. Barboncito told the President about the problems his people were having at Hwéeldi and asked him to let his people return to their traditional land. President Johnson listened and agreed to send representatives to Fort Sumner for a meeting with Navajo leaders in May.

Barboncito felt something important was about to happen. When the headman returned to Hwéeldi, he began getting ready for the American visitors. He and other medicine men held ceremonies that would help persuade the Americans to let the Navajos return home.

In late May, 1868, American visitors arrived at Fort Sumner led by General Tecumseh Sherman. Sherman was a famous Civil War general. Agent Dodd showed the general and his group around Bosque Redondo and Sherman was horrified by what he saw. He wondered how anybody or anything could live there. After his tour of Hwéeldi, Sherman asked to meet with Navajo leaders.

"BPF-Sherman, General Wm. T.," photographer unknown, engraving from daguerreotype, COURTESY OF THE COLORADO HISTORICAL SOCIETY, #33657

When Dodd told them of the meeting, the Navajo leaders met to choose one headman who would speak for them all. They all agreed that Barboncito was the best choice. People admired him for how well he spoke to people at meetings. The medicine men quickly held a ceremony for Barboncito, blessing him and giving his words power to persuade General Sherman.

In the morning of May 28th, the American and Navajo leaders met. Using interpreters, General Sherman asked Barboncito to tell him everything he could about Navajo life at Hwéeldi. He stood up. The time had come. He whispered a prayer to himself and began to speak. He told about how poor, sick, hungry, and sad his people were. He described how many Navajos had died and how many had just disappeared. Barboncito explained that the land at Hwéeldi wasn't meant for his people. The Navajo gods expected them to live among their sacred mountains.

General Sherman listened politely. When Barboncito's speech had been translated, Sherman took out a map of Navajo land. The general showed Barboncito boundary lines marked on the map and promised that, if the Navajos wished it, all the land inside the boundaries would be reserved for the Navajos forever. Then he suddenly asked Barboncito if the Navajos would want a reservation in Oklahoma Indian Territory, instead. He explained that many Indian tribes lived there, the land was good, and the Navajos would be safe from their traditional enemies. Barboncito was shocked. Hadn't General Sherman heard what he'd said?

"Unidentified Navajo man, Bosque Redondo era, ca. 1864-68," photographer unknown, COURTESY OF THE MUSEUM OF NEW MEXICO, #38202

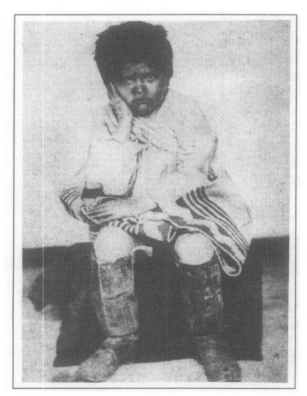

"Boy captive, Bosque Redondo, New Mexico," photographer unknown, COURTESY OF THE ARIZONA HISTORICAL SOCIETY, #14949

Before he could answer, the general added: "Yet if you wish to go back to your own land, you must live in peace. The Army will do the fighting for you. If you promise this, you may return to your own country."

When Sherman's words were translated, a thrill ran through the crowd of headmen.

"I hope to God you will not ask me to go back to any other country except my own!" Barboncito replied. "It might turn out to be another Bosque Redondo. When we came, we were told this was a good place, but it is not."

General Sherman nodded. Before ending the meeting, he asked Barboncito to choose ten headmen for their next two meetings. Together, the Navajos and the Americans would discuss making one last treaty.

On June 1, 1868, General Sherman called one last meeting behind the Bosque Redondo Indian hospital. Barboncito and his council of headmen sat with Sherman and his group of Americans. Thousands of Navajos quietly gathered in the fields surrounding the meeting place. Sherman held the new treaty in his hands. During their meetings, the general and the headmen had already agreed on what was written in the treaty. Still, General Sherman read each treaty promise out loud again and asked the Navajo leaders if they agreed.

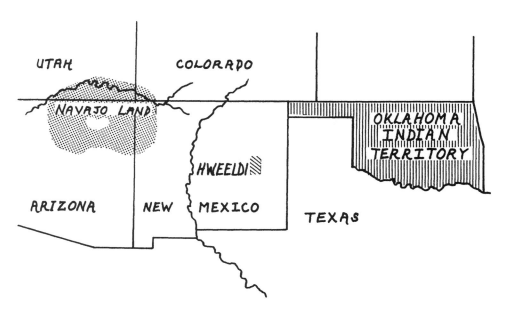

MAP 13: Oklahoma Indian Territory

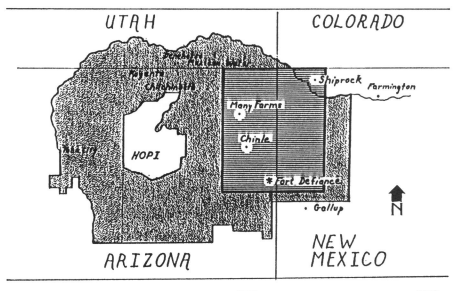

NAVAJO RESERVATION · 1868 ▦   NAVAJO RESERVATION TODAY ▨

MAP 13: The Navajo reservation in 1868 compared to the Navajo reservation today.

"Shall war between the United States and the Navajo Nation end?

"Shall the Navajo reservation belong to the Navajos forever?

"Will the Navajos stop raiding their enemies?

"Shall the Americans build schools and find teachers for Navajo children?

"Will the Navajo people send their children to school?

"Shall the Americans buy fifteen thousand sheep, five hundred cattle and one million pounds of corn seed for the Navajo people?"

Once more, Barboncito and the headmen agreed to each promise. General Sherman picked up a pen and signed the treaty. Then he handed the pen to Barboncito. Solemnly, he put his mark on the paper and passed the pen to Manuelito, then to Delgadito and the other headmen. Twenty-nine Navajo leaders signed the treaty. Barboncito's wish had come true. The Navajos were going home at last.

19 BEGINNING AGAIN

*"When we saw the top of the mountain from
Albuquerque, we wondered if it was our mountain
and we felt like talking to the ground, we loved it so.
Some of the old men and women cried with joy
when they reached their homes."*

—MANUELITO

"Jesus' wife and children," photo by Ben
Wittick, COURTESY OF THE MUSEUM OF NEW
MEXICO IN THE SPECIAL COLLECTIONS LIBRARY,
NORTHERN ARIZONA UNIVERSITY, #NAU-41723

On June 18th, seventeen days after signing the Treaty of
1868, eight thousand Navajos, with their two thousand sheep and
one thousand horses, began the long trip back to their homeland.
The line of Navajos was so long that they were only able to walk
ten to twelve miles a day. It was a hard trip, but a happy one.
Crossing the plains, the Navajos passed through the mountains
near Santa Fe, then journeyed southward towards Albuquerque.
There they waded across the Rio Grande River and headed westward towards Mount Taylor. When the people first spotted their
sacred mountain, many of them cried. Others sang songs of joy.
After traveling for more than a month, the Navajos were once more
in their traditional homeland.

Although they had returned to their native land, the Navajo
people knew life wouldn't be easy. Most families had little or no
livestock left. Their homes were in ruins and weeds filled their corn
fields. There were no seeds to plant and no tools for farming. In
spite of these problems, many Navajos went to their old homesites
to begin rebuilding. Many other Navajos settled near Fort Defiance, instead, to wait for the sheep, corn seed, and farm tools that
the Americans had promised to send them. While they waited,
these families lived much as they had lived at Hwéeldi. They put up
tents and small brush-covered shelters around the fort and survived
off of rations of beef, flour, salt, baking powder and sugar that the
Americans handed out to them. The months passed and the
Navajo people patiently waited. Still, no sheep arrived.

Over a year passed. At last in the fall of 1869, the promised
livestock arrived. The Americans drove fourteen thousand sheep
and one thousand goats to Fort Defiance. As the news of their
arrival spread, families began gathering at the fort. Before long,

nine thousand-five hundred Navajos arrived to collect their animals. The Americans gave many families only two sheep: one ram, or male sheep, and one ewe, or a female sheep. Those two sheep would be enough for each family to start a new herd. The Navajos drove the animals away to their homes. They didn't care where the Americans had said their reservation boundaries were. The Navajos headed straight to their old homes. They returned to Chinle and up to Black Mesa. They went north to Mexican Water and Oljato and west to Navajo Mountain. They traveled south to Dook'o'osłííd and resettled along the Little Colorado River. As they watched their flocks grow, the Navajo people remembered Barboncito's wise advice.

"Ration Day, Fort Defiance, 1874," photographer unknown, COURTESY OF THE SMITHSONIAN INSTITUTION IN THE SPECIAL COLLECTIONS DEPARTMENT, UNIVERSITY OF UTAH LIBRARIES, #2

"Now you are beginning again.
Take care of your sheep,
As you would care for your own children.
Never kill them for food.

If you are hungry,
Go out!
Find the wild plants,
Find the wild animals,
Or go without food,
For you have done that before!

These few sheep,
Must grow into flocks.
So that we,
The People,
Can be as we once were."

"Navajo, Manuelito Chonii, Carlisle, Pennsylvania, ca. 1880," photograph by John N. Choate, COURTESY OF THE MUSEUM OF NEW MEXICO, #59723

Afterword

The signing of the Treaty of 1868 ended the Navajo wars, but not the Navajo struggle for survival. The years following the Navajos' return to their traditional homeland were filled with hardship, yet the Navajo people were determined to regain and preserve their lives. With surprising speed, they resettled their lands, regained their herds, and recovered their culture and traditions.

All this they accomplished in spite of many obstacles. Rather than butcher their few sheep for food, the Navajos lived off government rations or lived off the land, much as their hunting and gathering ancestors had so many years before. As Navajo herds grew, the Navajo reservation expanded. Recovery was a rough road at times. There were conflicts with white ranchers in Arizona and New Mexico. Drought and severe winters also plagued the people and their stock. The Americans continued their attempts to change Navajo culture. The government forced children to leave their homes and attend distant boarding schools in hopes of wiping out the culture. The Bureau of Indian Affairs pressured Navajo leaders to accept foreign ways of government and business. After the government Stock Reduction Program destroyed half of Navajo sheep, goats and horses during the 1930s, many Navajo families had little choice but accept wage work as a way to earn a living.

Yet true to their nature, with each disaster the Navajo rebounded. Today there are over two hundred thousand Navajos living on a reservation the size of West Virginia. Livestock remains an important part of Navajo life. Government schools failed to end Navajo culture or the Navajo language. Navajo traditions and religious ceremonies remain strong. Today, Navajo government and Navajo businesses are an important influence in the Southwest. Navajos are in tribal and state governments. Navajo coal fuels the electrical needs of Phoenix, Albuquerque, Las Vegas and Los Angeles. In reservation border towns and large metropolitan areas, businesses have come to depend on Navajo consumers. In the face of seeming insurmountable obstacles, the Navajo have forged a nation, hammered out by the steady, level-headed determination, and fierce independence that so well defines a great people.

Appendix A

NAVAJO PRONUNCIATION GUIDE

Navajo, to the English speaker, is a very difficult language to learn and pronounce. It has many sounds that are not in English. It is also a tonal language, which means that the sound of vowels often are high or low, such as notes in a simple song. It also uses nasal sounds, made through the nose, as if you had a cold when saying that particular sound! Below is a list of Navajo words found in the book and a pronunciation guide that may help. The ['] over a vowel means make that sound one note higher. The [̨] under a sound means say it a little bit through the nose.

NAVAJO	PRONOUNCIATION	TRANSLATION
Adilohii	[ah-di-low-hee]	Rope Thrower, Kit Carson
Asdzą́ Biwoo' Adiní	[ahs-zah-bi-wo-ah-din-uh]	Lady No Teeth
Asdzą́ Diné Anaa'í	[ahs-zah-di-neh-aw-naw-uh]	Enemy People Woman
Bi'éé'Łichíí'ii	[bi-ay-thli-chee-ee]	His Red Shirt, Henry Dodge
Bikee' Dijool	[bi-kay-di-joal]	Round-Footed Girl
Bilagáana	[billah-gah-nah]	Americano, American
Bit'ahnii	[bit-ah-nee]	Under His Cover Clan
Dibé Ntsaa	[di-beh-nt-saw]	Mt. Hesperus, Colorado
Diné Anaa'í	[di-neh-aw-naw-uh]	Enemy Navajos
Dinébito'	[di-neh-bi-twoh]	The People's Waterhole
Dinétah	[di-neh-taw]	Among the Navajo, old Navajoland
Dook'o'ǫslííd	[doe-koe-ohs-leed]	San Francisco Peaks, Arizona
Hashkéneiniihii	[Hawsh-keh-nay-nee-hee]	Angrily Hands Them Out, Hoskininii
Hastiin Ch'ilhaajinii	[haws-teen-ch-ilha-jin-ee]	Black Plants Place Man, Manuelito
Hastiin Dághaa'	[haws-teen-daw-gaw]	Mr. Mustache, Barboncito
Hwéeldi	[whell-dee]	Fort Sumner
Mą'iideeshgizhnii'	[maw-ee-dish-gizh-nee]	Coyote Pass People Clan
Naabaahii	[naw-baw-hee]	Warrior, Narbona
Naahooyéí	[naw-hoe-yay]	Sweet potatoes
Naat'áanii Náádleeł	[not-aw-nee-nod-lailth]	Becomes Leader Again, Zarcillos Largos
Sisnaajinii	[sis-nah-gin-ee]	Mt. Blanca, Colorado
Tá'chii'nii	[taw-cheet-nee]	Red Streaked Earth Clan
Tábąąhá	[tah-baw-hah]	Water's Edge Clan
Tótsohnii	[twoht-soh-nee]	Big Water Clan
Tséhootsoí	[seh-hote-so-ih]	Wide Rock Area,
Tsoodził	[sowd-zilth]	Mt. Taylor, New Mexico
Yeiibicheii	[yay-bi-chay]	Grandfather of the Gods

Appendix B

"THE LAND WILL CATCH FIRE"
Memories of Fort Sumner

The following stories were related by Mrs. Nedra Todacheenie of Narrow Canyon, Arizona, as told to her by her maternal grandmother, Asdzą́ Biwoo' Adiní.

My maternal grandmother used to tell me about these things. While she was talking to us, if we went to sleep because we were lazy, she would say, "You shouldn't sleep! Run out and dash up a hill because our enemies are springing up around us! It is terrible to have enemies. When I was little our enemies were the Utes, the Mexicans, and the Pueblos. Almost everyone was our enemy, when I was raised here. They would come even at night!

"Here they come! The Utes are coming! Let's flee, even though snow covers the ground!"

Then they would run with their things packed on their backs, herding their goats and sheep before them for a great distance to chase them behind a hill. This is the way in which I was brought up. But look at you. You're luckier. Your clothes are heavier, thicker. You wear shoes that last. You have shoes and clothing, but when we were small we didn't have any of these. The only things we had were the things which we weaved for ourselves. This is how we were brought up," she said.

How is it that we had enemies? The Mexicans were already our enemies, they say. The Pueblos were, too. They must have been related to each other because the Mexicans used to move in with the Pueblos. Then they would settle on other people's land. They weren't too bad, it is said, but the Utes, as they are called, and the Comanches were really mean. They were the ones who almost ate us up, it is said. In eight years they had run everyone out of the area. There was nobody left.

There were some white men who came from Fort Defiance. There were about four white men who came. They said to us, "Go. Move to Fort Sumner. That is the only way you will survive. Terrible things will happen when they kill you off. What happened long ago will happen again, they say, when they kill you off. Because of you a big war has broken out and the earth will probably burn. The land will catch fire. That is why you should move to Fort Sumner . . . Over there are many kinds of enemies, but they already have their own enemies. They will probably consider you enemies also,

"Nedra Todacheenie, ca. 1972," photograph by Ken Hochfield, COURTESY OF KEN HOCHFIELD AND THE CALIFORNIA STATE UNIVERSITY, FULLERTON ORAL HISTORY PROGRAM.

but the soldiers will protect you from them. So all of you move over there."

This, they said to us over at Fort Defiance.

My grandmother said that long after many people had already gone, somebody named Biighaanii (His Back), said, "People have already moved!" Then they hurriedly moved to Fort Defiance. When they got there they found seven wagons in a row, long wagons with four huge horses hitched to each one. "So these are what they call wagons!" Somebody came over and told us that these were what we would use to travel by. "I'll be leading you," he said. Our grandmother told us that they led them, meandering, into the strangest places. It took us the entire winter to move to Fort Sumner. They arrived there in about springtime. It was warm over there, although it was the season for cold weather. Early in the morning when the soldiers would eat, the heat of the sun made steam rise from the little amount of snow which remained.

It is said that there was a river. Across from that river, there lived white people who were giving the Navajo supplies. It was just like food distribution we have here today. My grandmother said they gave away shoes, clothes, and gray blankets to the women. For the men they gave axes, shovels, picks, and saws like those which we have today. Each woman also received pans and cooking utensils. So all the old wood-burned dishes they had were tossed out.

The aspen wood would be partially hollowed out by fire and these would be used for dishes, such as pans. They were usually smeared with mud. It is said that it happened like this. Then food was distributed. They gave flour, wheat flour and potatoes. They also gave meat — baloney. Some people didn't know what kind of meat it was, so they threw it away! They didn't know any better then. Some of the people who had never seen flour before were asking, "How do you eat this?" Some just mixed the flour and water into a mush and ate it by licking it up!

This is how we were told by our grandmother.

They also gave coffee, which was unground and handed out in small sacks. They also gave out sugar, which was a little yellow. Somebody told them, "This is called sugar. First you cook it and then grind it up. Then you use a small amount of it in the coffee."

Your great grandmother cooked the sugar carelessly, grinding it up with grinding stones. When the family sat down to eat and drank the coffee with some of the prepared sugar, they began to spit it out. It was so bitter! "I don't know how it's fixed! Just forget it!" she said. Then they gave corn, which we had used in our foods and with which we were already familiar. As for the sugar, it was just used in liquids which we drank as we licked up the flour and water mush. We did the same with coffee. It is said they also gave out potatoes. At least they taught us how to prepare them, and we used them in stews. They told us that the meat we received was to be used with the potatoes in a stew.

There was a certain lady of a certain tribe who was called Asdzą́ Diné Anaa'í, Enemy Navajo Woman. They gave us this story. Some white men came over to her to show how to make bread. They told her to put baking powder in the flour.

"This is how you make it. This is what you make it with," they said.

Then they mixed it into a dough and brought out a grill. The lady who watched cried, "Eiya! That thing looks like the image of a spider! If you eat off that, you'll swell up! You're not supposed to use that!"

The white men said, "That's not so! They're just wires woven together. Put this over hot coals and cook the bread on top of it." Then they gave them frying pans. The Navajos cooked tortillas in them. They felt better not having to cook right on the grill. The Navajo didn't have a name for potatoes then, so they named them naahooyéí or sweet potatoes. My grandmother used to say, "Why don't you cook some naahooyéí'?"

I laugh at it now. It is said that this is what happened.

By this time the ones who came earlier to Fort Sumner had spent five years there. There, the women were given shoes, as were the boys. The men were also given shoes, a pistol, and knives. After four years they were told to move back to their former homeland. Somebody said, "Now you will move back to your homeland. To the east, right below the sunrise, lies Washington. There sits a man who has great power over the land. He has as much power as a man can have. No other person has nearly as much power as he. So right now all of you will move back to your homeland."

That was what the Navajos were told. The women cried joyously for the return to their homes, but some said, "What do you mean my land? Our land isn't very good! When we were taken away to Fort Sumner our enemies were devouring us! We had turned our heads away from the land." Some Navajos said these things. "When we came here, some of our problems were solved."

That is what happened.

Courtesy, Utah State Historical Society
and California State University, Fullerton
Oral History Program
Southeastern Utah Project
O.H. 1223 July, 1972

"Ti-co-ba-sha, Son to Chief Barboncito, ca. 1860s,"
photographer unknown, COURTESY OF THE SMITHSONIAN
INSTITUTION NATIONAL ANTHROPOLOGICAL ARCHIVES, #55767

Appendix C

Barboncito's Speech to General Sherman
at Fort Sumner, (*paraphrased*)

May 28, 1868

"I Want to Go See The Land Where I Was Born"

Bringing us here has made many of us die, also a great number of our animals. Our Grandfathers had no idea of living in any other place except our own land and I don't think it is right for us to do what we were taught not to do. When the Navajo were first made, First Woman pointed out four mountains and four rivers that was to be our land. Our grandfathers told us to never move east of the Rio Grande River nor west of the San Juan River. I think that because of this so many of us and our animals have died here. First Woman gave us our land and made it especially for us. She gave us the whitest corn and the best sheep and horses.

You can see our headmen here, as ordinary as they look, but I think that when the last of them is gone our world will come to an end. It's true we were brought here. It's also true that we have been taken care of well since we came here. As soon as we got here, we started working on irrigation ditches. I myself went to work with my men. We made all the fort buildings you see here. We always did as the soldiers told us to do. But this ground does not give crops. Every time we plant, nothing grows. All the stock we brought here has nearly died. We worked as hard as we could, but for nothing. That is why we haven't planted or tried to do anything this year. The plants never grow more than two feet high. I don't know why, only I think this land was never meant for us, even though we know how to plant and raise livestock. The General can see for himself that we have hardly any sheep or horses left, and we are so poor that we cannot buy any others.

There were many of us who were once rich and well off. Now they have nothing in their houses to sleep on except gunny sacks. It's true some of us have a little stock, but not near what we had years ago in our own country. For that reason my mouth is dry and my head hangs in sorrow to see those Navajos who were once so well off, but poor now. When we lived in our own way, we had plenty of stock. We had nothing to do but just look at our stock grow and when we wanted meat, all we had to do was kill it. These headmen were once rich. I myself feel sorry at the way I am here. I cannot sleep at night. I am ashamed to go to the fort store for my food. It is like I must depend on someone to hand it out to me. Since the time I was very small, I had my mother and father to take care of me. I had plenty. I always followed my father's advice to live in peace.

I want to tell the General that I was born in Canyon de Chelly. Now we have been living here for five years. The first year our corn crop was destroyed by worms. The second year it was the same. The third year it grew two feet high when a hail storm completely destroyed all of it. We have done everything we could to raise a crop of corn and pumpkins, but we were disappointed. I used to think at one time that the whole world was just like my own land, but I fooled myself. Outside my own country, we cannot raise a crop, but in it we can grow food almost anywhere. Our families and livestock get larger. Here they get smaller. We know this land does not like us. Neither does the water. I think it is true what my grandfathers said about crossing out of my own country. It seems that everything we do here causes death. Men working in the ditches get sick and die. Some die with the hoe still in their hands. Some to go the river to get water and suddenly disappear under it. Others have been struck and torn to bits by lightning! When a rattlesnake bites us here, it kills us. In our own country the rattlesnake would give us a warning so we could stay out of its way. If it bit us, we easily found a medicine for it. Here there are no plants for medicine.

When one of our headmen dies, the crying women make tears roll down onto my moustache. Then I think about my own country. When we first came here, there were mesquite roots to burn for firewood. Now there isn't any for twenty five miles around. During the winter, many die from cold and sickness and from working too hard carrying firewood such a long way on their backs. For that reason we cannot be happy here. Some years ago I could lift my head up and see flocks of cattle in every direction. Now I feel sorry I can't see any. I raise my head and see herds of stock on my right and left, but they are not mine. It makes me sorry when I think of the time I had plenty. I can barely stand it. All the different peoples around us are against us, the Mexicans and other Indian tribes. That is because we work hard and if we had the tools we could be much better off than either the Mexicans or other Indians. The Comanches are against us. I know, for they came here and killed a good many of our men. In our own land, we knew nothing about the Comanches.

Last winter I heard that you were coming here. Now I am happy you are here and I am waiting to hear why you came. I thank the General and I think of him like I think of my father and mother. As soon as I heard you were coming, I made three pairs of moccasins and I wore out two pair waiting for you. As you see, I am strong and healthy. Before I am sick or older, I want to go see the place I was born. Now I am just like a woman. I am sorry like a woman in trouble. I want to go and see my own country. If we are taken back to our land, we will call you our father and mother. If you would only tie a goat there, we would all live off it. We all feel the same. I am speaking for all Navajos and for their children who aren't born yet. All you hear me say is the truth. I hope you will do all you can to help us. I am speaking to you General Sherman as if you were a holy spirit. This hope goes in at my feet and out of my mouth. I wish you would tell me when you are going to take us to your own country.

I hope to God you will not ask me to go anywhere except my own country. If we go back, we will follow whatever orders you give us. We do not want to go right or left, but straight back to our own land.

Bibliography

Published and Unpublished Materials

Bailey, L. R.: *The Long Walk: A History of the Navajo Wars*, Westernlore Publications, 1978.

Brugge, David: Navajo History Manuscript; events in Navajo history around the Cebolleta area, late 18th and early 19th century, unpublished personal manuscript. No date given.

Bulow, Ernest: *Navajo Taboos*, Southwesterner Books, Gallup, New Mexico, 1982.

Charley, F. and D. Sundberg: *Interview of Kitty At'iinii*, O.H. 1224, July 13, 1972, Utah State Historical Society and the California State University, Fullerton Oral History Program, Southeastern Utah Project, Fullerton, California, 1973.

Interview of Nedra Tódích'ii'nii, O. H. 1223, July 13, 1972, Utah State Historical Society and the California State University, Fullerton Oral History Program, Southeastern Utah Project, Fullerton, California, 1973.

Clark, LaVerne H.: *They Sang for Horses: The Impact of the Horse on Navajo and Apache Folklore*, University of Arizona Press, Tucson, Arizona, 1966.

Connelley, William C.: *Doniphan's Expedition and the Conquest of New Mexico and California*, W. E. Connelley, Topeka, Kansas, 1907.

Correll, Lee J.: *Through White Man's Eyes*, Navajo Times Publishing Company, Window Rock, Arizona, 1976.

Davis, W. H.: *El Gringo, or New Mexico and Her People*, Rydal Press, Santa Fe, New Mexico, 1938.

Dozier, Edward: *The Pueblo Indians of North America*, Holt, Rinehart and Winston, Inc., 1970.

Driver, H., editor: Comparative Studies of North American Indians, American Philosophical Society, 1957.

Evers, Larry, ed.: *Between Sacred Mountains: Navajo Stories and Lessons from the Land*, Sun Tracks and the University of Arizona Press, Tucson, Arizona, 1984.

Frink, Maurice: *Fort Defiance and the Navajos*, Pruett Press, Boulder, Colorado, 1968.

Haile, Berard: *Head and Face Masks in Navajo Ceremonialism*, St. Michael's Press, St. Michael's, Arizona, 1947.

Hoffman, Virginia: *Navajo Biographies, Volume I*, Navajo Curriculum Center Press, 1974.

Johnson, B.: *Navajo Stories of the Long Walk Period*, Navajo Community College Press, Tsaile, Arizona, 1973.

Kelly, Lawrence: *Navajo Roundup: Selected Correspondence of Kit Carson's Expedition Against the Navajo, 1863-1865*, Pruett Publishing Company, Boulder, Colorado, 1970.

Kipp, David: *Tse'Laa', The Incredible True Story of Navajo Fortress Rock*, David F. Kipp, Chinle, Arizona, 1983.

Kluckhohn, Clyde, *Navaho Witchcraft*, Beacon Press, 1944.

The Navaho, Doubleday and Company, revised, 1962.

Navaho Material Culture, Harvard University Press, 1971.

Link, Martin *Navajo: A Century of Progress, 1868-1968*, The Navajo Tribe, Window Rock, Arizona, 1968.

Locke, Raymond *The Book of the Navajo*, Mankind Publishing Company, 1976.

McNitt, Frank, *Navajo Wars: Military Campaigns, Slave Raids and Reprisals*, University of New Mexico Press, Albuquerque, New Mexico, 1972.

Newcomb, Franc J.,: *Hosteen Klah: A Navajo Medicine Man and Sand Painter*, University of Oklahoma Press, Norman, Oklahoma, 1975.

Roberts, Calvin and Susan: A History of New Mexico, University of New Mexico Press, Albuquerque, 1986.

Roessel, Robert: *Dinétah, Navajo History, Volume II*, Navajo Curriculum Center, Rough Rock Demonstration School, Rough Rock, Arizona, 1983.

Pictorial History of the Navajo From 1860 to 1910, Navajo Curriculum Center, Rough Rock Demonstration School, Rough Rock, Arizona, 1980.

Schaafsma, Polly: *Rock Art in the Navajo Reservoir District*, Museum of New Mexico Press, Papers in Anthropology #7, Santa Fe, New Mexico, 1971.

Spicer, Edward: *Cycles of Conquest: The Impact of Spain, Mexico, and the United States on the Indians of the Southwest, 1533-1960*, University of Arizona Press, Tucson, Arizona, 1972.

Sturtevant, William C.: *Handbook of North American Indians*, Smithsonian Institution, Washington, D. C., 1984.

Terrell, John: *The Navajos: The Past and Present of a Great People*, Harper and Row Publishers, 1970.

Twitchell, Ralph E.: *The Leading Facts of New Mexican History*, Sunstone Press, 2007

Thompson, Gerald: *The Army and the Navajo: The Bosque Redondo Reservation Experiment, 1863-1868*, University of Arizona Press, Tucson, Arizona, 1982.

Underhill, Ruth: *Here Come the Navajo!*, United States Department of the Interior, Division of Education, Bureau of Indian Affairs, Washington, D. C., 1953.

United States Government: *Treaty Between the United States of America and the Navajo Tribe of Indians*, K.C. Publications and the Navajo Tribe, 1968.

Wilson, John: *Fort Sumner, New Mexico*, Museum of New Mexico Monuments Division, 1967.

Yazzie, Ethelou, ed.: *Navajo History*, Navajo Curriculum Center, Rough Rock Demonstration School, Rough Rock, Arizona, 1982.

Young, Robert: *The Role of the Navajo In the Southwestern Drama*, The Gallup Independent and Robert W. Young, 1968.

Young, R. and W. Morgan: *The Navajo Language: A Grammar and Colloquial Dictionary*, University of New Mexico Press, Albuquerque, New Mexico, 1980.

INDEX